SIGNIFICANT AMERICAN MUSICIANS, COMPOSERS And SINGERS

Childrens Press
Chicago, Illinois

CREDITS

EXECUTIVE EDITOR
IDA S. MELTZER, B.S.
Vice Principal
Marine Park Jr. High School
Brooklyn, New York

CONSULTANTS
JACK KENT MANDEL, M.B.A.
John Wilson Jr. High School, Brooklyn, New York

JANET TEGLAND, M.A.
Saddleback Community College, Mission Viejo, California

RESEARCH AND PRODUCTION
THOMAS McLAUGHLIN

ROBERT GOLDIN

JOSEPH POSTILION

NICK CURCIO

RONALD FALK

Library of Congress Cataloging in Publication Data
Main entry under title:

Significant American musicians, composers, and singers.

Includes index.
SUMMARY: Brief biographies of 183 musicians, composers, and singers arranged in chronological-alphabetical order.
1. Musicians, American—Biography—Juvenile literature. [1. Musicians] I. Title: Musicians, composers, and singers.
ML3930.A2S484   780'.92'2 [B] [920]   75-20691
ISBN 0-516-05306-X

© 1975 Regensteiner Publishing Enterprises, Inc. Excerpts from works entitled People Who Made America are included by permission under © 1973 United States History Society, Inc., Skokie, Illinois

Table of Contents

Pages

Early Period (1815-1860) 7-9

Second Period (1861-1899) 10-13

Third Period (1900-1939) 14-18

Fourth Period (1940-1969) 19-46

Contemporary (1970-   ) 47-77

CUSHMAN—EMMETT

Charlotte Cushman

Daniel D. Emmett

Cushman, Charlotte S. Praised for the strength and clarity of her voice, Charlotte Cushman, playing both male and female roles, rose to international popularity as an actress and singer in the mid-1800s. Born in Massachusetts in 1816, Miss Cushman was trained by her mother for a career in opera and at the age of 19 won a featured role in *The Marriage of Figaro*. Turning her talents to acting, Miss Cushman at once demonstrated a unique and versatile talent. She toured England from 1845 to 1849, playing leading male parts in *Romeo and Juliet, Hamlet,* and *Henry VIII*. A popular leading lady, Miss Cushman returned to the United States for three years and won generous praise from both critics and audiences. She toured America and Europe from 1852 until 1870, then returned home to retire except for occasional dramatic readings of famous plays. Miss Cushman died in Boston, February 17, 1876.

Emmett, Daniel Decatur. Composer of "Dixie," the song Confederate army soldiers sang and marched to during the Civil War, Daniel Emmett started one of the first blackface minstrel groups in America and spent more than forty years popularizing minstrel music. Asked by the leader of the Bryant Minstrels to compose a "walk-around" song, Emmett in 1859 was inspired by a showman's phrase, "I wish I was in Dixie-land" to write the song that became famous. Two years later, shortly after the outbreak of the Civil War, "Dixie" was sung as the closing number at a concert in New Orleans and was received with great enthusiasm. It was chosen by soldiers and civilians as the unofficial anthem of the South.

Born in Ohio in 1815, Emmett composed his first song, "Old Dan Tucker," at the age of fifteen. Serving with the army in the 1830s as a fife player, he joined a traveling circus troupe after his discharge in 1835. Organizing the Virginia Minstrels in 1842, Emmett designed the group's colorful costumes of white trousers, striped calico shirts, and long, blue calico swallow-tail coats. Playing the banjo, bones, violin, and tambourine, the Minstrels made their first appearance at New York's Bowery Amphitheatre in 1843. They were a popular success and toured several American cities. Joining the Bryant Minstrels in 1857, Emmett composed several songs during the Civil War, including "The Road to Richmond," "Here We Are, or Cross Over Jordan," and "Walk Along John." After the Civil War, he again toured the U.S. Emmett died in 1888.

FOSTER—FRY

Stephen Foster

William H. Fry

Foster, Stephen C. Composing many of America's most popular ballads, including "My Old Kentucky Home" (1853) and "Old Black Joe" (1860), Stephen Foster recorded in folk music the emotions of average people in the 1800s. Many of his most celebrated songs were written in the everyday language of the southern black. Black and white minstrels sang his tunes for more than a century, and many of his songs won popularity throughout the U.S.

Born in Pennsylvania in 1826, Foster attended college in the 1840s but devoted most of his talents to composing music. His earliest songs included "Tioga Waltz" (1840) and "Open Thy Lattice, Love" (1844). In 1846 Foster's parents sent him to Cincinnati to work for his brother, an accountant. After several of his ballads were published in 1848, including "O Susanna," "Camptown Races," and "Away Down South," Foster returned to Pennsylvania determined to become a professional songwriter. The following year, the singing group Christy's Minstrels popularized his ballad, "Nelly Was a Lady." In 1851 Foster sold the Minstrels the right to sing his songs before they were published. During the next few years they sang his ballads before hundreds of audiences. Between 1851 and 1860 Foster composed many of his most popular songs: "The Old Folks at Home" ("Swanee River"), "Massa's in de Cold, Cold Ground," "Beautiful Dreamer," "Old Dog Tray," and "Jeanie With the Light Brown Hair." After moving to New York in 1860, Foster composed few memorable songs and fell into debt. He died in 1864.

Fry, William H. Composer of the first opera written by an American, William Fry in 1845 laid the foundation for music appreciation in the United States. His opera *Leonora* featured a cast of 140 singers and musicians and followed the Italian opera style, with emphasis on recitatives, arias, and chorals. When criticized for his overuse of the Italian style, Fry led a crusade to rally support for American artists in their struggle to create an American operatic style. To stimulate greater interest in music and encourage music appreciation, Fry in 1852 and 1853 lectured at New York's Metropolitan Hall on voice, musical instruments, and variations in classical music forms.

Born in 1813 in Philadelphia, Fry began writing music for piano at the age of 14 and composed his first overture as a student at Mount St. Mary's preparatory school. For several years he studied under composer Leopold Meignen and by the age of 20 had published three additional overtures. Although Fry was a serious student of music, his chosen profession was journalism, and in 1829 he began working for his father's newspaper, *The National Gazette*. After the production of *Leonora*, Fry spent six years in Europe as a foreign correspondent for the *New York Tribune*. Returning to the U.S. in 1852, he pioneered music criticism in America as the *Tribune's* music editor. Fry's other compositions include the opera *Notre Dame de Paris* and the symphonies *A Day in the Country*, *Santa Claus, or the Christmas Symphony*, and *Childe Harold*. William Fry died in the West Indies in 1864.

GILMORE—GREENFIELD—LANIER

Patrick S. Gilmore　　**Elizabeth Greenfield**　　**Sidney Lanier**

Gilmore, Patrick Sarsfield. A colorful military band leader who believed the bigger the band, the better the music, Patrick Gilmore organized the biggest bands of the 19th century. Born in Ireland in 1829, he went to Canada in 1846 as a cornet player with an Irish regimental band, then formed his own band in Salem, Massachusetts and toured the U.S. During the Civil War, Gilmore was in charge of all army bands in Louisiana and in 1863 wrote words and music for "When Johnny Comes Marching Home." In 1864 he began to test his theory that big bands make better music by conducting a chorus of 5,000 and a "monster" band of 500 pieces supported by drummers and artillery. By 1872, he was conducting a band of 2,000 and a chorus of 20,000 accompanied by cannon, church bells, and Boston firemen beating the "Anvil Chorus" on 50 anvils. Gilmore died in St. Louis in 1892.

Greenfield, Elizabeth Taylor. A soprano called the Black Swan because of her singing voice, Elizabeth Greenfield in the 1850s became the best-known black concert artist of the middle 19th century. It was said her voice range covered thirty-one full, clear notes. Born a slave in Mississippi in 1809, Elizabeth as an infant was moved to Philadelphia where she was adopted by a Mrs. Greenfield, a Quaker. Discovering Elizabeth's singing talent, Mrs. Greenfield arranged for her music lessons. First appearing at private parties, Miss Greenfield in 1851 made her public debut in Buffalo, New York, where her ability as an artist was quickly recognized. While making a tour of England in 1854, Miss Greenfield was honored with an invitation to perform at Buckingham Palace for Queen Victoria. After a brief career, Miss Greenfield retired to manage a voice studio in Philadelphia. She died in 1876.

Lanier, Sidney. Believing that poetry should be written in musical rhythms, poet-musician Sidney Lanier created one of the most original verse styles in 19th century America. His most popular poem is "The Marshes of Glynn." Born in Georgia in 1842, Lanier learned to play several musical instruments as a child. After graduating from Oglethorpe College in 1860, he joined the Confederate army. Lanier's first and only novel, *Tiger Lilies* (1867), describes his imprisonment during the Civil War. For several years Lanier worked as a teacher, and in 1873 he joined Baltimore's Peabody Orchestra as a flutist. He first won national recognition for "Corn" (1874) and "The Symphony" (1875), two poems contrasting the agricultural life of the South with the industrial North. His collected poems were published in 1877 and his musical theory of poetry in *The Science of English Verse* (1880). Lanier died in 1881.

BETHUNE—HOWE—KELLOGG

Thomas G. Bethune Julia Ward Howe Clara Louise Kellogg

Bethune, Thomas Greene. A blind slave, Thomas Bethune developed his musical talents and memory to become a popular pianist and composer in the late 1800s. Born in Georgia in 1849, Tom, along with his mother, was sold to a Colonel Bethune, whose name Tom adopted. Still a child, he surprised his new owner by playing some difficult piano selections which he had heard others perform. From then on, Bethune was allowed full use of the piano. He was able to play any music that he heard, and in time, his selections included Bach, Beethoven, Chopin, and his own compositions. The colonel brought Bethune to Savannah, Georgia for his first recital, advertising him as "Blind Tom, the Marvelous Musical Prodigy." As his popularity rose, bringing wealth to the colonel and his family, Bethune performed in Europe, at the White House, and throughout several states, until shortly before his death in 1908.

Howe, Julia Ward. An author, reformer, and crusader for women's rights, peace, and the abolition of slavery, Julia Ward Howe is best remembered for the song "The Battle Hymn of the Republic," published in 1862. She wrote the stirring words while visiting an army camp near Washington, D.C. and set them to the tune of "John Brown's Body." "The Battle Hymn of the Republic" became the semiofficial war song of the Union army during the Civil War. Born in 1819 in New York, Miss Ward received her education in private schools. In 1843 she married educator and reformer Samuel Gridley Howe and joined him in the antislavery movement. A writer of poetry and essays, her biography of author and reformer Margaret Fuller (1883) was considered one of her finest literary accomplishments. A pioneer in the fight for women's right to vote, she was an official of peace organizations. Mrs. Howe died in 1910.

Kellogg, Clara Louise. Organizing her own opera company in 1873, soprano Clara Kellogg for 20 years attempted to popularize Italian and French opera sung in English. Appearing as Marguerite in the first New York presentation of *Faust,* Miss Kellogg became closely identified with the role. The opera was usually sung in Italian, and to present it and other operas in English, she not only translated the texts, but also arranged the stage settings and trained the principals and chorus. Miss Kellogg was always careful to maintain the highest traditions of Italian and French operatic singing. Born in South Carolina in 1842, she studied singing in New York and made her debut at the Academy of Music as Gilda in Verdi's *Rigoletto.* A dramatic soprano, Miss Kellogg advanced the cause of operas sung in English. Her book *Memoirs of an American Prima Donna,* an autobiography, was published in 1913. She died in 1916.

Edward A. MacDowell

Ethelbert Nevin

MacDowell, Edward Alexander. Pianist and composer Edward MacDowell first gained recognition when composer Franz Liszt arranged in 1882 to have his piano concerto *First Modern Suite* performed in Switzerland. Born in New York in 1861, MacDowell began his musical studies at an early age and continued his work abroad in France and Germany. At the age of 21, his concerto was performed in Switzerland, encouraging him to compose songs, sonatas, and symphonic poems. Returning to the U.S., MacDowell composed more works. Some of his most widely performed compositions include *Indian Suite* (1892) and *Woodland Sketches* (1896). He was invited to organize a music department in 1896 at Columbia University. Failing to have his liberal ideas of music study accepted by the university and his students, MacDowell resigned in 1904. He died in New York City in 1908.

Nevin, Ethelbert W. Among the first composers to show an individual American style, Ethelbert Nevin in the late 19th century composed simple songs of joy which attained large popularity. His song "Narcissus," from a group called *Water Scenes*, in 1891 became a world favorite. His song "The Rosary" in 1898 became the most popular by an American since the works of Stephen Foster. Born in 1862 near Pittsburgh, Nevin was introduced to the piano by his mother when he was five, and at eleven he played in a public concert. His parents took him to Europe when he was fifteen to study for a year, but when Nevin later announced his intention of becoming a professional musician, his father objected. After overcoming opposition of his parents, he studied under several teachers at home and abroad, determined to become a concert pianist. After five years of concert work and composing, he found himself turning more and more to the composing of music.

Nevin's *Sketch Book*, a collection of songs and piano pieces, established his reputation at the age of 26. He achieved international recognition with *Water Scenes,* and he followed it with *In Arcady* (1892), *May in Tuscany* (1896), and *A Day in Venice* (1898). Altogether Nevin wrote and published more than 130 compositions, most of them songs, but some were written only for piano, violin, or chorus. Music authorities attribute Nevin's talent to his ability to write words and couple them with light and bright melodies. Nevin died in 1901 while working on a cantata, *The Quest*.

PAINE—PARKER—RITTER

John Knowles Paine   Horatio W. Parker   Frederic Ritter

Paine, John Knowles. Known for composing symphonies and choral works in the late 1800s, organist John Paine founded the first university music department in the United States at Harvard University in 1872. When the university increased its choice of liberal arts subjects in the 1870s, Paine added courses in musical theory and history, and in 1875 he became one of the first professors of music. Born in Maine in 1839, Paine studied in Berlin. He returned to America in 1861 and became a leading organist. In 1862 he was appointed music director at Harvard. Paine was chosen to write the special music for the opening of world fairs at Philadelphia in 1876, Chicago in 1893, and St. Louis in 1904. His works captured the style and rhythm that were popular at the turn of the century. Paine's contribution to music teaching influenced many later American composers and critics. He died in 1906.

Parker, Horatio William. A medieval Latin poem inspired Horatio Parker in 1893 to compose *Hora Novissima,* a musical composition for chorus, soloists, and orchestra that brought him acceptance as the most celebrated American composer of the late 19th century. Teaching at Yale University, he exercised a far-reaching influence on American music. Born in Massachusetts in 1863, Parker at nineteen went to Germany to study. On his return he taught at the Cathedral School in Garden City, Long Island and at the National Conservatory in New York. After the success of *Hora Novissima,* Parker was selected choir director at Trinity Church in Boston and professor of music at Yale. For the next 25 years he continued to teach music and was associated with a variety of musical activities. He composed two operas with poet Brian Hooker: *Mona* and *Fairyland.* Parker died in 1919.

Ritter, Frederic. A gifted composer, conductor, and educator, Frederic Ritter played a leading role in awakening Americans in the 1850s to appreciate the listening pleasure of classical music. Founder of the Cincinnati Philharmonic Orchestra and professor of music at Vassar College for almost a quarter of a century, Ritter also wrote several significant books on musical history, including *Music in America* in 1883. Born in Strasbourg, Alsace in 1834, he immigrated to the United States in 1856, settling in Cincinnati. As director of the Cincinnati Philharmonic and the Cecilia Society Choral Group, he presented outstanding programs of classical music. His musical influence was expanded during the Civil War when he moved to New York to direct concerts. His own compositions, including several symphonies and concertos, were played by orchestras in New York and Boston. Ritter died in 1891.

SEIDL—THOMAS—THURSBY

Anton Seidl **Theodore Thomas** **Emma Thursby**

Seidl, Anton. Closely associated with some of the most outstanding composers of the 19th century, conductor Anton Seidl greatly influenced American taste for classical music by introducing the works of European composers in the U.S. He presented the operas of Richard Wagner to American audiences and also conducted the first American performance of Anton Dvorak's *New World Symphony* in 1893. Born in Hungary in 1850, Seidl studied music at the Leipzig Conservatorium and was chosen by Wagner to help arrange the Bayreuth Festival of Music in 1876. Named a conductor of the Metropolitan Opera, he made his first American appearance in 1885 conducting *Lohengrin*. He became a naturalized American citizen in 1891 and conducted both the Metropolitan and the Philharmonic Society orchestras. He was also editor in chief of *Music of the Modern World*. Seidl died in 1898.

Thomas, Theodore. The founder of the Chicago Symphony Orchestra in 1891, conductor Theodore Thomas awakened the American public's interest in many new composers. Born in Germany in 1835, Thomas made his first public appearance as a violinist at age six and in 1845 was brought to America by his parents. He played first violin in an orchestra that accompanied many well-known operatic performers in the early 1850s, including Jenny Lind. Thomas organized his own orchestra in 1862 and between 1864 and 1878 conducted symphony concerts in New York. He founded the Wagner Union in New York in 1872 and did much to popularize the works of Wagner in America. Appointed conductor of New York's Philharmonic Society in 1877, Thomas led that group throughout the 1880s. He resigned from the Philharmonic in 1891 to organize the Chicago Symphony. Thomas died in 1905.

Thursby, Emma Cecilia. One of the first classical American singers to win recognition in Europe, soprano Emma Thursby was considered among the foremost interpreters of Mozart during the 19th century. Miss Thursby spent many years on the concert stage. She then became a voice teacher and helped guide the careers of several talented singers, including Geraldine Farrar, a widely acclaimed soprano. Born in Brooklyn, New York in 1845, Miss Thursby, whose voice reached an extraordinary range (from middle C to high F), studied voice in Italy as well as in the United States. She first appeared as a concert singer at the Bedford Church in Brooklyn in 1875. Though refusing to sing opera, she gave concerts on tours in Europe and the U.S. and won wide critical and popular praise. After touring the Orient in 1903, she retired to devote herself to teaching. Miss Thursby died in 1931.

ARTEAGA—BLAND—BURLEIGH

Julio C. de Arteaga **James Bland** **Harry T. Burleigh**

Arteaga, Julio C. de. A world celebrated pianist in the late 19th and early 20th centuries, Julio Arteaga won recognition as one of Puerto Rico's most original composers of concert music. Born in Puerto Rico in 1867, Arteaga came to the U.S. at age 14 to advance his musical education. He soon traveled to Paris to continue his studies at the French National Conservatory of Music from 1882 to 1888. Arteaga moved to Cuba two years later to become director of the National Conservatory in Havana. During the next twenty years, he performed in New York City, taught at New York's International Conservatory of Music, and formed groups in the Academy of Music and Choral Society in San Juan. He presented a *Musical Review* in Puerto Rico in 1907 and later introduced works by Chopin, Debussy, and Rachmaninoff. Arteaga gave his last recital at Carnegie Hall in New York City in 1922. He died in 1923.

Bland, James. A black banjo-playing minstrel, James Bland entertained audiences in England and the United States at the turn of the century and composed many of America's favorite songs, including "Carry Me Back to Old Virginny," later adopted as the Virginia state song. One of the first blacks to become a popular minstrel, Bland broke into an entertainment field in which whites often impersonated blacks. Born in 1854 in New York, Bland attended Howard University and soon decided on a career in music. After his popularity as a composer and minstrel grew in America, he toured England, where he was invited to perform in almost every major theater. His earnings reportedly were $1,000 a week. Bland returned to the U.S. in 1907 to discover that minstrels were no longer popular. Composer of "Oh, Dem Golden Slippers" and "In the Evening by the Moonlight," Bland died a pauper in 1911.

Burleigh, Harry Thacker. Singer, composer, and arranger Harry Burleigh reflected his black heritage in his music and introduced traditional spirituals to the concert stage in the late 19th and early 20th centuries. Born in Pennsylvania in 1866, Burleigh sang in choirs and obtained a scholarship to the New York National Conservatory of Music. There he studied with composer Anton Dvorak and was selected over 50 applicants to be the baritone soloist at a predominantly white Episcopal church. He was also selected as choir soloist at a Jewish temple. Singing his own compositions and the spirituals of his ancestors, Burleigh toured America and Europe. In 1917 he won the NAACP Spingarn Medal for excellence in creative music. Before his death in 1949, Burleigh had composed more than 90 songs and over 50 choral pieces and arranged about 50 spirituals, including "Deep River."

COHAN—FOY—HAMMERSTEIN

George M. Cohan   Eddie Foy   Oscar II and Oscar I Hammerstein

Cohan, George Michael. Known as Yankee Doodle Dandy, playwright, actor, and songwriter George M. Cohan, beginning in the late 1800s, entertained American audiences with his lively performances and patriotic songs for more than 45 years. He composed many famous tunes, including "I'm a Yankee Doodle Dandy," "You're a Grand Old Flag," and "Give My Regards to Broadway." His song "Over There," written for American troops during World War I, brought Cohan a special congressional medal years later in 1940. Born in Providence, Rhode Island in 1878, Cohan performed with his family on the vaudeville stage. He later wrote and starred in many patriotic plays and won a leading role in Eugene O'Neill's drama *Ah, Wilderness*. After almost a half-century as a leading entertainer and talented composer, Cohan died in 1942. His life story is dramatized in the movie *Yankee Doodle Dandy*.

Foy, Eddie. After a colorful performing career as a dancer, singer, and comedian for almost 50 years, Eddie Foy in 1913 organized his seven children to form one of America's most popular vaudeville troupes. Born Edwin Fitzgerald in New York in 1856, he began dancing at the age of seven. He moved to Chicago in 1865 to become an actor. After changing his name to Eddie Foy in 1872, he began a career of singing and dancing with a show traveling through mining towns and cities in the West. Foy returned to Chicago in 1888 and was soon featured in several comedy plays, including *Bluebeard* (1888) and *Hotel Topsy Turvy* (1898). From 1913 to 1923, Foy and his children performed in vaudeville. With faces painted like clowns, the Foys entertained hundreds of audiences with songs, dancing, and comic routines. After a brief retirement, Foy appeared in a drama, *The Fallen Star*. He died in 1928.

Hammerstein: Oscar I and Oscar II. Both Oscar Hammerstein I, during the late 1800s, and his nephew Oscar Hammerstein II, during the mid-1900s, were major forces in advancing the music theater in America. Born in Germany around 1847, Hammerstein I moved to the U.S. in the 1860s. He began managing, building, and buying theaters and helped popularize grand opera in the English language by charging low prices to appeal to large audiences. He died in 1919. Oscar II was born in New York in 1895 and graduated from Columbia in 1916. A lyricist and playwright, he wrote many musicals stressing strong story lines and romantic characters. He was credited by critics with advancing the art form of musical theater. With Richard Rogers, he wrote lyrics and stories for shows produced on stage, film, and television. His most popular are *Oklahoma!*, *Carousel*, and *South Pacific*. He died in 1960.

HERBERT—JOPLIN

Victor Herbert

Scott Joplin

Herbert, Victor. A gifted cellist and later conductor of the Pittsburgh Symphony Orchestra, Victor Herbert in the late 19th and early 20th century won acclaim as America's outstanding composer of light operas. Born in 1859 in Ireland, Herbert at the age of seven was sent to Germany to study music, and at twenty-three he became first cellist in Johann Strauss's orchestra in Vienna. In 1886 Herbert came to America as first cellist at New York's Metropolitan Opera. He became conductor of the Pittsburgh Symphony Orchestra in 1898 and in 1904 began conducting Victor Herbert's New York Orchestra, which became nationally popular. Herbert's prominence was of real assistance when in 1909 he led the successful fight for favorable copyright legislation for composers. He also was a founder of the American Society of Composers, Authors, and Publishers (ASCAP) in 1914.

Herbert's career as a composer began with *Prince Ananias,* a light opera produced in New York in 1894. Its instant popularity encouraged him to concentrate on other light operas, and he composed many throughout his lifetime. Herbert's works include *Babes in Toyland* (1903), *Mlle. Modiste* (1905), which features the song "Kiss Me Again," *The Red Mill* (1906), and his popular *Naughty Marietta* (1910). He wrote the musical scores for several Ziegfield Follies and also composed two grand operas, *Madeleine* and *Natoma*. In 1916 he wrote the musical score for the film *The Birth of a Nation* and later composed music for other motion pictures. Herbert died in 1924.

Joplin, Scott. Originator of a lively style of music developed while playing piano in saloons, black composer Scott Joplin wrote the "Maple Leaf Rag" in 1899 and became recognized by many critics as the Ragtime King. A music publisher, John Stillwell Stark, heard Joplin play the song in the Maple Leaf Club and purchased the tune for fifty dollars plus royalties to the composer. The song sold hundreds of thousands of copies and helped popularize ragtime music throughout the country. Joplin's "Maple Leaf Rag" enabled performers to exhibit their playing ability in many forms of syncopation, and the song was used for years as a test of technique and style for ragtime pianists. Joplin and Stark became partners and wrote many popular tunes.

Joplin was born to a musical family in Texarkana, Texas in 1868 and began playing piano at seven. While in his teens, he joined a group of wandering musicians. He arrived in St. Louis in 1885 and while playing in small night clubs, perfected his ragtime piano style. Joplin's ragtime music continued to grow in popularity, but he became dissatisfied and attempted to compose in other musical forms. He wrote a short opera *A Guest of Honor, a Ragtime Opera,* and a ballet that were not favorably received. Later he moved to New York and wrote a complete opera, *Treemonisha,* which he published at his own expense. Unable to find a financial backer, he staged it without scenery or costumes and played all the orchestral parts himself. The show closed after one performance. Joplin died in 1917.

Chauncey Olcott   **Maud Powell**   **Leo Schulz**

Olcott, Chauncey (Chancellor John). Although a native of the United States, Chauncey Olcott made his musical reputation as an outstanding Irish singer on the American stage in the late 1800s and early 1900s. He introduced the popular Irish song "Mother Machree" and composed the ballad "My Wild Irish Rose." Born in Buffalo in 1860, Olcott made his first stage appearance at the Buffalo Academy of Music. In the 1880s he traveled with minstrel companies, playing in blackface, and later moved on to musical comedy. In 1891 he traveled to London to appear as an Irish character in a light opera. Returning to the U.S., he started a career in Irish musical plays that made him one of the most popular entertainers in the theater at the turn of the century. He retired after World War I, but returned in 1924 to play the Irishman Sir Lucius O'Trigger in the play *The Rivals*. Olcott died in 1932.

Powell, Maud. Considered by music critics to be one of America's outstanding concert violinists of the 19th century, Maud Powell gave her first professional concert in the United States at the age of seventeen. She was the first violinist to make records for the Victor Talking Machine Company in the early 1900s. Born in Illinois in 1868, Miss Powell was playing Mozart sonatas at age eight. Traveling to Europe in 1880, she studied with Charles Dancla in Paris and Joseph Joachim in Berlin. After returning to America, she made annual concert tours throughout the United States. She actively encouraged the work of new American and European composers and introduced many violin compositions to American audiences, including the Tschaikovsky Concerto in 1889. She also gave command performances for Queen Victoria, King Edward VII, and Czar Nicholas II. Miss Powell died in 1920.

Schulz, Leo. A child prodigy who made his musical debut at the age of five, Leo Schulz performed as soloist and first cellist of leading American orchestras for 40 years between 1889 and 1929 and became one of the world's most respected musicians. Born in 1865 in Poland, Schulz displayed unusual talent as a child. After studying at the High School for Music in Berlin, he became first cellist with the Berlin Philharmonic Orchestra in 1885 and in 1886-89 performed with the Gewandus Orchestra in Leipzig. He immigrated to the United States in 1889 and became first cellist of the Boston Symphony Orchestra. He became soloist and first cellist of the New York Philharmonic Orchestra in 1889 and continued with the orchestra until 1929. He was cellist for the Margulies Trio from 1904 to 1915. Appointed professor of music at Yale University, Schulz also composed many works for the cello. He died in 1944.

SOUSA

John Philip Sousa

Sousa, John Philip. Recognized as the March King of martial music, John Philip Sousa composed and orchestrated more than 100 marches in the late 1800s and early 1900s and became the outstanding influence on American band music. One of few men to serve in three branches of the U.S. military service, Sousa was conductor of the U.S. Marine Band from 1880 to 1892, musical director of the 6th Army Corps during the Spanish-American War, and director of all navy bands during World War I. Sousa was named director in 1880 of the U.S. Marine Band, which became noted for outstanding musicianship and precision marching. By his constant drilling, rehearsing, and strict discipline, the band soon was rated as the most distinguished of all military musical groups. Sousa's marches include "Washington Post March" (1899), "The Gladiator" (1888), "The High School Cadets" (1890), and "Stars and Stripes Forever" (1897). "Semper Fidelis" (1888) later became the official march of the United States Marine Corps.

Sousa was born in Washington, D.C. in 1854 and showed an early interest in music. At the age of six he entered a conservatory to study violin and at the end of three years won all five medals awarded by the school. He also learned to play several band instruments. He enlisted in the U.S. Marine Band at thirteen and played with the band for five years. In 1872 he conducted an orchestra at Kernan's Theater Comique in Washington, D.C. and was also hired as a violinist in the orchestra playing at Ford's Opera House. He began composing music and published a few songs including "The Review." During the Philadelphia Centennial Exhibition of 1876, he was the violinist with Jacques Offenbach's orchestra. After directing the U.S. Marine Band, Sousa resigned in 1892 to form his own band.

Although he hired the most talented musicians available and trained them in his musical and precision marching styles, Sousa's band received little attention at first; but by 1893 the band was one of the most popular in America. They performed at many events, including the Chicago World's Columbian Exposition in 1893. The band traveled throughout the U.S. and Europe and from 1910 to 1912 gave concerts throughout the world.

In addition to marches, Sousa wrote ten comic operas, including *El Capitan* (1896), *The Bride-Elect* (1897), and *The Free Lance* (1906). He also wrote three novels and an autobiography. Sousa died in 1932.

ARMSTRONG

Louis Armstrong

Armstrong, Louis. Titled America's musical ambassador to the world, Louis Armstrong with his appealing personality and impressive musicianship became known all over the world in the years 1930 to 1970. With his unusual jazz style, lively wit, and gravel voice, he fascinated audiences on three continents with his joyous trumpet and singing. During a career of almost half a century, Armstrong and his band played in remote areas of Africa, as well as in all Western countries and Russia, captivating audiences on every tour. His triumphs included a command performance in 1934 before King George VI of England. He was enthusiastically received.

Born in 1900 in New Orleans, Armstrong was sent to a reform school when he was 13 and learned to play a cornet and bugle after his musical interest was aroused by cornetist Buck Jones. Armstrong became leader of the school band. On his release, he sold newspapers and delivered milk and coal and in the evenings received trumpet lessons from his idol, King Oliver. Armstrong was nicknamed Satchmo (for satchel mouth) as a tribute to the power that he blew into his trumpet and joyous sounds that flowed from his mouth when singing his own "scat" style. In 1922 he joined Oliver for engagements in Chicago. By 1924 he was playing with bands that included Fletcher Henderson and Erskine Tate, before forming his first band, the Hot Five, in 1926. Within three years, Armstrong had a worldwide reputation.

Publicized as the "world greatest trumpeter," Armstrong began making jazz and blues recordings, which were soon in great demand. These include "Chinatown," "I Can't Give You Anything But Love," "Shine," "Tiger Rag," "I'll Walk Alone," "C'est Si Bon," "Ain't Misbehaving," and "When the Saints Go Marching In." Armstrong's infectious grin and singing style brought him many motion picture offers. He and his band appeared in film musicals with many featured singers and dancers of the 1940s, 50s, and 60s and cut records in combination with almost every popular singing artist. This helped enlarge his reputation as the industry's most unusual and popular singer of songs.

Armstrong made his first trip abroad in 1933, playing in France, Italy, Switzerland, Norway, Holland, and England. He visited Europe and Africa in 1956 and newsreels of the tour were released under the title of *Satchmo the Great*. In 1969 he performed before thousands of jazz lovers in several cities of the Soviet Union and received a wildly enthusiastic welcome. Armstrong died in New York in 1971.

BECHET—BRICE—CANTOR

Sidney Bechet   Fannie Brice   Eddie Cantor

Bechet, Sidney. Black jazz clarinetist Sidney Bechet performed to 20th century audiences around the world and helped preserve the musical style called New Orleans jazz. Bechet was one of the first jazz musicians to be accepted as a serious artist by classical musicians. Born in New Orleans in 1897, Bechet, as a young man, played his clarinet and soprano saxophone in King Oliver's jazz band. While touring with Cook's Southern Syncopated Orchestra in 1919, he brought the "New Orleans sound" to England and the continent. A command performance before the king of England brought fame to Bechet and his solo, "The Characteristic Blues." Returning to the U.S., he made records with Clarence William's Blue Five and played for a while with Duke Ellington. After another tour in Europe with Noble Sissle's band, Bechet formed his own trio. He later settled in Paris, where he died in 1959.

Brice, Fannie. With songs, jokes, and a Yiddish accent, comedienne Fannie Brice entertained America from the early 1900s to 1951. She turned the songs "Sadie Salome" and "Second-Hand Rose" into classics of American humor. Fannie was born in New York in 1891. Although she won a prize for her version of "When You Know You're Not Forgotten by the Girl You Can't Forget," Miss Brice was fired by George M. Cohan from a dancing chorus line. Soon after, Florenz Ziegfeld found her singing in a New York City burlesque show and paid her $75 a week to perform in the Ziegfeld Follies. She became a featured singer and won national fame with the song "My Man." Miss Brice later appeared in the movie *Be Yourself* and created the radio character Baby Snooks, a little girl heard nearly every week until Fannie's death in 1951. The stage musical and the movie *Funny Girl* are based on Miss Brice's life.

Cantor, Eddie. An entertainer who became one of America's most popular and highly paid attractions in musical comedies, motion pictures, radio, and television, impish song and comedy celebrity Eddie Cantor used his talents to raise over $250 million for many humanitarian causes. Born Edward Iskowitz in 1892 in New York, Cantor started his career on street corners and rose to theatrical prominence in the Ziegfeld Follies (1917-1919) and *Whoopee* (1928). Cantor appeared in many motion picture comedies including *The Kid from Spain* (1932) and *Ali Baba Goes to Town* (1937). He entered radio in 1931 and by 1936 was the highest-paid performer. During World War II he aided war bond and Red Cross drives. His participation in the March of Dimes attracted millions of contributors. Cantor's television career started in 1950. He was also a popular author. Cantor died in 1964.

Nat "King" Cole

John Coltrane

Cole, Nat "King" (Nathaniel Adams). The first black performer with his own national television show (1956), Nat "King" Cole won wide acclaim as a singer, pianist, and writer of popular music. Critics praised his sincere lyrics and smooth, effortless singing style. Born in 1919 in Alabama, Cole at the age of five moved to Chicago with his family. He received his musical education from his mother, a church choir director. Before Cole established his own trio in 1936, he played in a black revue called *Shuffle Along* and later as a jazz pianist in Hollywood nightclubs. Cole's first recording in 1943, "Straighten Up and Fly Right," sold half a million records. His other popular hits include "Nature Boy" and "Chestnuts Roasting on an Open Fire." In the 1940s he became the only black performer to have his own network radio program and later his own national television show (1956-57). He died in 1965.

Coltrane, John. One of America's most imitated black jazz musicians, John Coltrane, beginning in the 1960s, developed the practice of the extended solo, often playing up to 45 minutes of uninterrupted music. Coltrane believed that music should express man's deepest emotions and his sound was described as "screeching, blasting, and free." He began his solo with a simple melody, which he repeated over and over, and then varied the melody into clusters of shrill notes. One critic remarked, "The saxophone in Coltrane's hands becomes a human voice in full cry."

Born in North Carolina in 1927, Coltrane was deeply influenced by the hymns and gospel music heard in black southern churches. He first learned music while playing with a small Philadelphia group in the 1940s. Later he performed with a navy band and a rhythm and blues group. Before organizing his own jazz quartet in 1960, Coltrane performed with many leading jazz musicians, including Thelonious Monk, Miles Davis and Dizzie Gillespie. After concert tours in Europe and Japan, Coltrane returned to the U.S. and in 1965 was voted Jazzman of the Year by *Downbeat* magazine. His first popular recording was his rendition of "My Favorite Things." Coltrane also recorded many albums, including *Blue Train*, *A Love Supreme*, and *Ascension*. He once stated his philosophy: "My goal is to live a truly religious life and to express it through my music. I'd like to point out to people that music transcends words. I want to speak to their souls." Coltrane died in New York in August 1967, at the age of 40.

DETT—ELLINGTON

Robert Dett

Duke Ellington

Dett, Robert Nathaniel. Arranging hundreds of Negro spirituals into concert music, pianist and composer Robert Dett during the 1920s and 30s created a new and heightened appreciation of the religious music of black Americans. Dett's most popular works were called motets and oratorios—musical compositions of stories with biblical themes. His oratorio *The Ordering of Moses*, published in 1936, continued to be popular with leading concert groups in America and Europe in the 1970s. As a spokesman for black music, Dett in 1920 excited the interest of academic and critical audiences with his scholarly essay "The Emancipation of Negro Music," a work he composed while at Harvard.

Born in Quebec, Canada in 1882, Dett earned a music degree from Oberlin College in 1908. He later studied at other universities, including Harvard, Columbia, and Pennsylvania. After touring the U.S. as a concert pianist, Dett in 1913 was appointed director of music at Hampton Institute in Virginia. Remaining at Hampton for 15 years, Dett led the institute's choir on a tour of Europe and the U.S. during the early 1930s. After several years of composing and concert appearances, Dett began his collection of Negro spirituals. Dett's many compositions include *The Enchantment Suite* (1922), his choral arrangement of *Listen to the Lambs,* and the motet *The Chariot of Jubilee* (1921). His four-volume work in music history, *Dett Collection of Negro Spirituals* (1936), was considered by music critics as a rich and authentic source of basic American music. He also composed music for radio programs. Dett died in 1943.

Ellington, Duke (Edward Kennedy). Blending smooth melodies with unusual harmony and rhythmic effects, composer and musician Duke Ellington pioneered modern jazz in the first half of the 20th century. Born in 1899 in Washington, D.C., Ellington turned down an art study scholarship to play his music around Washington and New York City. By the late 1920s, he had won a reputation as one of America's top black musicians and composers. Ellington's band continued to perform regularly in nightclubs and in many of the world's most important concert halls. Over the years, Ellington won almost every musical honor, including popularity polls and awards given by critics. He wrote almost 1,000 tunes, including "Mood Indigo," "Sophisticated Lady," and "The A Train." He won the Spingarn Award of the NAACP in 1959 and the Presidential Medal of Honor in 1969. Ellington died in 1974.

FARRAR—GARDEN—GARLAND

Geraldine Farrar **Mary Garden** **Judy Garland**

Farrar, Geraldine. An operatic soprano who became internationally famous in the early 1900s, Geraldine Farrar was one of the youngest Americans ever chosen to sing a leading role with the Metropolitan Opera. She was also the first American operatic artist to achieve critical acclaim in Germany. Born in Massachusetts in 1882, Miss Farrar studied music in Italy and Germany, making her initial appearance at the age of 19 as Marguerite in a Berlin production of *Faust*. Chosen to sing Juliette in *Romeo et Juliette* at the Metropolitan in 1906, she later became well known for her outstanding performance as Madame Butterfly. Miss Farrar retired in 1922, but later formed her own road company. Appearing in several motion pictures, her best known films are *Carmen, Joan of Arc,* and *The Woman and the Puppet*. Her autobiography, *Such Sweet Compulsion,* was published in 1938. Miss Farrar died in 1967.

Garden, Mary. Considered one of the most talented dramatic opera stars at the turn of the 20th century, Mary Garden was chosen by the composer Debussy to sing the role of Mélisande at the first performance of his opera *Pelléas et Mélisande* in Paris in 1902. Born in Aberdeen, Scotland in 1877, Miss Garden moved to America with her family when she was six. After taking voice lessons in Chicago for several years, she went to Paris in 1895 to study with Trabadello and Fougère. She sang her first role, *Louise*, at the Opéra Comique in Paris in 1900. Returning to the United States in 1907, she made her first American appearance at New York's Manhattan Opera House and joined the Chicago Grand Opera Company in 1910. She became director of the Chicago Opera Association in 1921. After her retirement, Miss Garden returned to Scotland in 1944. She died in Aberdeen in 1966.

Garland, Judy. A leading box office attraction in film musicals and in dramatic roles during the 1940s and 50s, Judy Garland won international popularity as one of America's dynamic singers and actresses. She first won acclaim for her leading role in the motion picture *The Wizard of Oz* (1938) and was awarded a special Academy Award for singing "Somewhere Over the Rainbow." Born Frances Gumm in Minnesota in 1922, she was raised in a family of vaudeville performers. After her performance in *Oz*, she costarred in the popular Andy Hardy series. She later appeared in 35 film musicals, including *Meet Me in St. Louis* and *The Easter Parade*. During the 1950s, Miss Garland's concerts set attendance records at London's Palladium and later at New York's Palace Theater. During the late 1950s and early 60s she appeared in feature roles in many motion pictures and on television. Miss Garland died in 1969.

GERSHWIN—GROFE

George Gershwin

Ferde Grofe

Gershwin, George. Introducing a striking variation of melody into the popular tunes of the 1920s and 30s, pianist and composer George Gershwin created a new type of sophisticated music called symphonic jazz. Many critics agreed that Gershwin's *Rhapsody in Blue* (1924) opened a new era of musical experimentation in America. His *Rhapsody* was described as "a piano concerto derived from blues and jazz." A popular composer and song writer, and a talented conductor and soloist as well, Gershwin also wrote the internationally acclaimed folk-opera *Porgy and Bess* (1936), which includes the popular songs "Summertime" and "It Ain't Necessarily So."

Born in Brooklyn in 1898, Gershwin studied in the public schools on New York's East Side. At the age of 16 he left high school to pursue a musical career and became a pianist for a music publisher. After joining a new company in 1918, Gershwin composed his first successful song "Swanee," later popularized by Al Jolson. Acclaimed as a composer with a new and fresh sound, Gershwin was soon commissioned to write musical scores for New York theaters. With his brother Ira, who wrote the lyrics, Gershwin produced many popular Broadway musicals, including *Of Thee I Sing* (1932), the first musical comedy to win a Pulitzer Prize. His concert music includes the *Concerto in F* (1925), for piano and orchestra. The symphonic poem *An American in Paris* (1928) blends popular French tunes with original music. After his death in Hollywood in 1937, Gershwin's music grew in popularity.

Grofe, Ferde. For more than 50 years a leading musician of a style called symphonic jazz, pianist, violinist, composer, and conductor Ferde Grofe, beginning in the 1920s, created new sounds that helped describe the character of people and places in America. Giving his music a lively carefree beat, Grofe combined strong jazz rhythms with the slower and more structured harmony of symphonic arrangements. His most popular symphony, *The Grand Canyon Suite* (1929), drew a musical picture of the vast Rocky Mountain ranges. He varied the rhythm and harmony of the music to represent the changing geography of the mountains.

Born in New York City in 1892, Grofe learned to play many musical instruments from his parents. At the age of 17 he became a violinist for the Los Angeles Symphony Orchestra. During the 1920s Grofe joined Paul Whiteman's band as a pianist and arranger. His arrangement of Gershwin's "Rhapsody in Blue" increased Whiteman's popularity and started the new trend in music experimentation called symphonic jazz. After forming his own dance band in the 1930s, Grofe became a featured attraction at leading supper clubs throughout the country. He later conducted a weekly radio program that featured the popular music of the 1940s. During his 50-year career, Grofe composed more than 200 musical works, including *The Death Valley Suite, Symphony in Steel*, and *Kentucky Derby*. Before he died in 1972, Grofe stated his philosophy of composing music: "Inspiration is like a little bird. If you don't grab him, he flies right out the window."

GUTHRIE—HANDY

Woody Guthrie

W. C. Handy

Guthrie, Woody. Folksinger, guitarist, and composer Woody Guthrie, during the mid-1900s, roamed the country to tell through music his story of America's accomplishments and failures. Born in 1912 in Okemah, Oklahoma, Guthrie witnessed a series of tragedies in his family and in his teens left home to begin his travels. During his career, Guthrie wrote more than 1,000 songs, although he was unable to read music. The songs usually described his own experiences or what he witnessed in waterfront saloons, skid rows, and hobo jungles across the country. During the 1940s, Guthrie, with Pete Seeger and others, formed the Almanac Singers. The group traveled extensively throughout the United States and performed in many concerts, mostly to audiences made up of laborers. Among the many songs that Guthrie wrote are "This Land Is Your Land" and "Hard Traveling." Guthrie died in 1967.

Handy, William Christopher. Called the Father of the Blues, cornetist and composer W. C. Handy, beginning in 1912, helped popularize black folk music with his new and different orchestral arrangements. To the slow, moody melodies of the black folk songs, Handy added big band orchestration that featured cornets, trumpets, and saxophones. For its sad lyrics describing rejected love and the hardships of working in the cottonfields, his music was called "blues." Handy's most popular songs, "St. Louis Blues" and "Memphis Blues," led to the further development of jazz music in the late 1920s.

Born in Alabama in 1873, Handy received music lessons from a country fiddler and church cornetist. While attending school, he learned to play guitar and sang with a minstrel quartet. He formed his own group and traveled to Chicago in 1893 to perform at the Columbian Exposition. He later joined the Mahara Minstrels and by 1896 had established a national reputation as a cornet soloist. Beginning in 1900, he taught music at Alabama A & M College for two years and then returned to the Minstrels. Settling in Memphis, Handy formed a new band that popularized his unique blues sound. His "Memphis Blues" (1912) was the first composition of its style published in America. In 1918 Handy established a music company in New York City, publishing Negro hymns, spiritual, and records of blues music. His collections include *Blues: An Anthology* (1926) and *Book of Negro Spiritual Hymns* (1938). Retiring in the late 1940s, Handy died in New York City in 1958.

HAWKINS—HENDERSON—HERNANDEZ

Coleman Hawkins   Fletcher Henderson   Rafael Hernandez

Hawkins, Coleman. A pioneer in the developmen of jazz music, Coleman Hawkins beginning in the 1920s raised the saxophone to new importance as a versatile solo instrument. His saxophone style, featuring full, rich tones and a heavy vibrato, became the most widely imitated musical jazz sound for more than thirty years. Before Hawkins demonstrated the versatility of the saxophone as a solo instrument, it was used mostly for background melody and harmony. Born in 1904 in Missouri, Hawkins began playing the saxophone at the age of 9. He studied at Washburn College in Topeka, Kansas and in 1923 joined Fletcher Henderson's band and quickly began developing his solo style. During the 1930s, he toured Europe for five years, performing in concerts in almost every large city. Returning to the United States, Hawkins formed his own band. Hawkins died in New York City in 1969.

Henderson, Fletcher. Featuring a new music sound called "hot jazz," black pianist and bandleader Fletcher Henderson helped create the "big band" sound that became popular during the 1930s and 40s. His band also helped popularize the sound of the saxophone and tuba in jazz orchestration. Critics praised his skillful use of counterpoint techniques with brass (trumpet) and reed (saxophone) instruments, which he combined to play individual melodies at the same time. Born in 1898, Henderson graduated from Atlanta University and in 1920 began his musical career in New York as pianist for a music publisher. Two years later he formed a 10-piece jazz band. With arranger Don Redman, Henderson created unique improvisations and introduced his counterpart techniques. For more than 25 years his band played in leading night clubs throughout America. Henderson died in 1952.

Hernandez, Rafael. A musician and composer whose "El Jibarito," written in 1929, became an unofficial Puerto Rican anthem, Rafael Hernandez for 40 years was an important figure in Spanish-American music. Born in 1889 in Puerto Rico, he moved to New York before World War I. Having mastered the cornet, trombone, and banjo, Hernandez in 1925 began composing music and later formed a trio that played and sang throughout the United States, Cuba, Mexico, and Puerto Rico. "El Jibarito" is a patriotic outcry against the misery of colonialism. It gained wide popularity among Puerto Ricans, and Hernandez followed it with "Capullito de Aleli," a 1932 composition that also became a Spanish-American favorite. After recording more than 2,000 compositions and spending many years touring throughout Latin America, Hernandez returned to Puerto Rico, where he died in 1965.

Charles Ives

Mahalia Jackson

Ives, Charles Edward. For creating techniques that produced new and striking musical sounds, Charles Ives won recognition as one of the most original composers of 20th century music. He originated polyrhythms (contrasting rhythms), polyharmony (chords played in different keys), and atonality (the absence of key). Adding new freedom and dimension to serious music, Ives combined hymns, marches, and popular tunes into symphonies, sonatas, and chamber music. In describing the richness and complexity of Ives's music, one critic wrote that "no one seems able to find any kind of musical behavior that cannot be found in the music of Ives."

Born in 1874 in Connecticut, Ives graduated from Yale in 1898 and entered the insurance business. He later wrote: "A man could keep his music interests stronger, cleaner, bigger, and freer if he didn't make a living out of it." During the next 18 years Ives created many compositions in his spare time. Forced by illness to give up composing in 1917, he began publishing his manuscripts at his own expense. His Second Pianoforte Sonata—subtitled *Concord, Massachusetts, 1840-60*—was first performed in Germany in 1928. His *Three Places in New England* (1914) and *Decoration Day Music* (1912) were first performed in the 1930s. He was elected in 1945 to the National Institute of Arts and Letters, winning a Pulitzer Prize for his *Third Symphony*, a composition written in 1947. During his remaining years, Ives gained an international reputation and his compositions were played with renewed interest and enthusiasm. Ives died in 1954.

Jackson, Mahalia. Called Queen of the Gospel Song, black singer Mahalia Jackson in the 1940s began to popularize black gospel music in America. Until Miss Jackson's songs attracted attention from all races, most gospel music was heard mainly in black churches. Her recording in 1945 of "Move on Up a Little Higher" introduced a new rhythm to America and became the first gospel song to sell more than a million records. Critics praised her "great range and expressiveness" and ability to reach "the high falsettos and the rumbling lows; the gentle whispers and the shooting climaxes."

Born in New Orleans in 1911, Miss Jackson sang in her father's church choir as a child. Moving to Chicago in 1927, she worked as a hotel domestic until she had saved enough money to open a beauty shop. While singing with one of the city's church choirs, she established a local reputation and recorded her first gospel song, "God Gonna Separate the Wheat from the Tares" (1934). After she recorded "Move on Up," her popularity increased rapidly. During the 1950s, Miss Jackson made concert appearances throughout America and Europe, started a weekly radio program, and became a television guest performer. She was selected to sing the oration at Martin Luther King's funeral in 1968. Miss Jackson's albums include *Sweet Jesus Boy, The World's Greatest Gospel Singer,* and *Bless This House.* Before she died in 1972, she remarked: "Gospel singing is a heart feeling. It's also got to have His love, and that's what I've got to sing if I'm going to sing at all."

JOHNSON, J. Rosamond—JOHNSON, James

J. Rosamond Johnson

James P. Johnson

Johnson, J. Rosamond. Combining classical training with his own black musical heritage, J. Rosamond Johnson wrote "Lift Every Voice and Sing," considered by some as the black national anthem. He helped produce the first black musical comedies on Broadway in the early 20th century. Born in Florida in 1873, Johnson studied at the New England Conservatory of Music. Early in his career he traveled with a vaudeville company, taught music in Jacksonville, and wrote songs with his brother, James Weldon Johnson. In 1901 Johnson teamed with his brother and Robert Cole to write Broadway shows. Their most popular musical comedies were *The Shoo Fly Regiment* (1906) and *The Red Moon* (1908). Johnson served as director of Hammerstein's Opera House in London in 1912-13 and later taught in the U.S. He compiled the *Book of American Negro Spirituals* (1925). Johnson died in 1954.

Johnson, James P. A recognized jazz pianist and composer whose techniques in the 1920s were often copied by many popular musicians, James P. Johnson developed a unique musical style known as the "stride piano." Johnson's distinctive style stressed a strong left hand bass rhythm to add musical contrast to the melody. Born in New Brunswick, New Jersey in 1891, Johnson studied piano as a child with his mother and at 13 was playing ragtime music professionally. He developed his singular style in competition with other jazz pianists when he found that he could add liveliness and rhythm to an original melody by filling in the pauses with *glissandos* (a sliding movement), *tremolos* (a quivering effect), and other variations from the written music.

He spent hours listening to classical recordings, which enabled him to produce concert effects in his jazz playing and to transpose classical music to a ragtime style of jazz. Playing solo piano in night clubs and producing player-piano rolls and recordings, Johnson still found time to compose many popular songs in ragtime and blues rhythm. His "Carolina Shout" was called a test of the jazz pianist's skill. Johnson composed popular songs such as "If I Could Be with You," "Charleston," and "Old Fashioned Love." He composed songs for the musical comedies *Runnin' Wild* and *Keep Shuffling* and was musical director for *Plantation Days* and *Smart Set*. Later he turned to black music, composing *Symphonic Harlem* and *Symphony in Brown*. In 1945 an all-Johnson concert was performed at Carnegie Hall. He died in 1955.

JOLSON—KERN

Al Jolson

Jerome Kern

Jolson, Al. A singer and actor with a unique performing style that made him a favorite with generations of Americans, Al Jolson was the most popular stage entertainer in the U.S. during the early 1900s. After appearing in many successful Broadway musicals, including *Big Boy* (1921) and *Artists and Models* (1925), he played the feature role in the first major talking movie *The Jazz Singer* in 1927. Jolson went into semiretirement in the 1930s, making few public appearances, but during World War II, he entertained U.S. troops on every front in Europe and the Pacific area. After the war, he collaborated in writing the film version of his life story for two movies in the 1940s—*The Jolson Story* and *Jolson Sings Again*. Singing the sound track for the two movies, he again popularized his song hits of the 1920s— "Mammy," "Swanee," and "Sonny Boy."

Born Asa Yoelson in Russia in 1886, Jolson was the son of a Jewish cantor. He immigrated to the United States with his family in 1893. His first singing experience was in his father's synagogue choir in Washington, D.C. Despite his family's wish that he become a rabbi, Jolson became interested in the stage. After performing in circuses and vaudeville, he joined Lew Dockstader's minstrel troupe in 1909, and his appearance in blackface was so well received that the role became his entertainment trademark. In 1911 he sang in his first musical comedy on Broadway, *La Belle Paree*. Returning to the United States after entertaining American servicemen and women in Korea, Jolson died of a heart attack in 1950.

Kern, Jerome. By combining the style of American folk music with the lightness and tempo of Viennese operettas, Jerome Kern composed some of America's best-loved songs in the mid-1900s and created a uniquely different American musical form. Born in New York, January 27, 1885, Kern studied piano and music theory at New York College of Music and later in Germany. His first big musical was *Sally* (1920), written in collaboration with Victor Herbert.

In 1927 he wrote *Showboat*, his most successful musical comedy, which features such songs as "Ol' Man River," "My Bill," "Only Make Believe," and "Can't Help Lovin' That Man of Mine." From 1933 until his death in 1945, Kern composed musical scores for Fred Astaire and other actors. Among the songs he wrote for movies are "The Way You Look Tonight," and "A Fine Romance." With Oscar Hammerstein II he wrote "The Last Time I Saw Paris."

KREISLER—LEDBETTER—LEVANT

Fritz Kreisler   **Huddie Ledbetter**   **Oscar Levant**

Kreisler, Fritz. One of the 20th century's renowned violin virtuosos, Fritz Kreisler won international acclaim for his pure and distinct classical style. He was called a master of compact and flawless bow movement and unique vibrato sounds. His short compositions including *Caprice Viennois* and *Schon Rosmarin*, were highly popular. Born in Austria in 1875, Kreisler was first taught to play the violin by his father. At age 10 he won the gold medal of the Vienna Conservatory. While still in his early teens, Kreisler in 1888 made his first American tour. He then returned to Vienna and studied medicine. After his Berlin debut in 1899, Kreisler again toured the U.S. and in 1915 settled in New York. He published in 1935 a collection of compositions entitled *Classical Manuscripts*, which he said were written by 17th and 18th century composers. Later he revealed that all were his own creations. Kreisler died in 1962.

Ledbetter, Huddie (Leadbelly). Gifted with a unique singing style and a talent for composing folksongs, Huddie Ledbetter generated a widespread interest in American folk music in the 1940s that grew in popularity for decades. Known as Leadbelly, he was serving a prison sentence for manslaughter in Louisiana in 1934 when he sang some of his songs for musical historians Alan and John Lomax. Under their sponsorship, he was released from prison and helped them collect folksongs from prisons and small towns throughout the South. Born in Louisiana in 1888, Ledbetter learned to play the guitar as a child. After his release from prison, he toured the southern U.S. with the Lomaxes and appeared as a soloist on college campuses and in New York's Town Hall. He toured France in 1949. His most popular songs include "Good Night, Irene" and "On Top of Old Smoky." Ledbetter died in 1951.

Levant, Oscar. A sharp-witted humorist, musician, and composer, Oscar Levant in the 1940s gained a wide reputation as an author, classical pianist, movie actor, and radio quiz-show panelist. Born in 1906 in Pennsylvania, Levant studied piano and musical composition at an early age and later performed in New York and other cities. Going to Hollywood in 1928 as an actor, Levant also composed music for motion pictures. Tremendously impressed after his meeting with composer George Gershwin in 1929, Levant devoted himself to playing Gershwin's works almost entirely. Levant's remarkable memory and biting wit also made him a popular performer on radio. Between 1940 and 1952 he appeared in many movies and played numerous concerts. His compositions were played by symphony orchestras, and he wrote articles and books, including *A Smattering of Ignorance*. Levant died in 1972.

LUNCEFORD—McCORMACK—MELCHIOR

Jimmie Lunceford   **John McCormack**   **Lauritz Melchior**

Lunceford, Jimmie. Combining musical talent with outstanding showmanship, jazz bandleader Jimmie Lunceford influenced prominent orchestra leaders and musical arrangers during the 1930s and 1940s. Lunceford became an expert musician on all reed instruments, and his Lunceford style of jazz music was followed by many band leaders, including Sonny Dunham and Tommy Dorsey. Born in 1902 in Missouri, Lunceford graduated from Fisk University. After he became skillful in playing the saxophone and clarinet, he formed his first band in 1927. By 1934 Lunceford had attained wide recognition in the field of jazz arrangements. His band was accepted as one of the leading musical groups in America until 1942, when many of the original members left the band. His rhythmic style and musical brightness remained a guide for later jazz musicians. Lunceford died in 1947.

McCormack, John. Considered one of the most popular Irish tenors in Europe and America, John McCormack became the best-paid singer in the U.S. in the 1920s and 30s, earning more than four million dollars from his records and concerts. Born in Ireland in 1884, McCormack won first prize for his singing at the National Irish Festival in 1903 and made his first appearance as an operatic singer in Italy in 1906. Moving to America in 1909 to perform with the Boston, Chicago, and Metropolitan opera companies, he was widely praised by critics for his outstanding singing voice. He left his opera career in 1913 to devote his talents to the concert stage. During World War I, he appeared in concerts to raise money for war charities and bond drives and at the end of the war became a U.S. citizen. His most famous recording was "When Irish Eyes Are Smiling." McCormack retired in 1938 and died in 1945.

Melchior, Lauritz. Considered by music critics as the supreme Wagnerian tenor of his time, Lauritz Melchior sang leading roles at New York's Metropolitan Opera from 1926 to 1950. Born in Denmark in 1890, Melchior entered the Royal Theater's operatic school in 1913 and made his debut as Silvio in *Pagliacci*. He sang baritone for three years before becoming a tenor. Known to few opera directors in 1924, he was engaged to sing Siegfried in *Die Walküre* at a performance in London. Later singing in Bayreuth, the Wagner shrine in Germany, Melchior was heard by the conductor of the Metropolitan Opera and engaged to sing in *Tannhauser* for his American debut in 1926. His powerful voice was heard over loud orchestration, and he could reach high C without effort. Six feet, four inches tall and weighing 270 pounds, he was almost exclusively cast in Wagnerian operas. Melchior died in 1973.

MILLER—MILLS—MITROPOULOS

Glenn Miller　　**Florence Mills**　　**Dimitri Mitropoulos**

Miller, Glenn. One of the most popular bandleaders of the late 1930s and early 40s, Glenn Miller created an unusual sweet, smooth sound in his orchestra by combining a clarinet with four saxophones and balancing them with trombones and trumpets. He played dance music and songs, and his recordings of "In the Mood," "Moonlight Serenade," and other arrangements sold more than a million copies each. Miller was born in 1904 in Iowa. He began his musical career as a jazz trombonist, then became a music arranger for other band leaders. He formed his own band in 1937 but it was unsuccessful. The following year Miller established a new band, and it quickly won the acclaim of popular-music fans throughout America. Joining the army after the outbreak of World War II, he organized a military orchestra. Miller was aboard a plane that disappeared over the English Channel in December 1944.

Mills, Florence. A singer, dancer, and comedian, Florence Mills was one of the most popular entertainers of the 1920s. She performed in musical comedies and nightclubs, singing such songs as "I'm Just Wild About Harry" and her theme, "I'm a Little Blackbird Looking for a Bluebird." Born in 1895 in Washington, D.C., Miss Mills gave her first professional stage performance at the age of five in *Sons of Ham*. In 1910 she formed a singing trio with her sisters and appeared in musicals and vaudeville. Later she was the lead singer in a nightclub act, The Panama Four. When one of the leading actresses of the all-black musical *Shuffle Along* fell ill in 1921, Florence Mills replaced her. Her performance was an overwhelming success. The next year she was featured in the musical *Plantation Review*. She also performed in *From Dover to Dixie* and *Blackbirds*. Miss Mills died in 1927.

Mitropoulos, Dimitri. Conducting symphony orchestras without referring to the music and leading without a baton, musical director Dimitri Mitropoulos led many of America's symphonic orchestras between 1936 and 1958. Born in Greece in 1896, Mitropoulos studied piano and after graduating from the University of Athens in 1919 completed courses in organ and composition in Brussels and Berlin. Mitropoulos made his first appearance in America in 1936 as guest conductor of the Boston Symphony Orchestra. His performance brought him appointment as permanent conductor of the Minneapolis Symphony, where he remained until 1949. In 1950 he was appointed musical director of the New York Philharmonic Symphony Orchestra and conducted the orchestra until 1958. A champion of contemporary music, he often featured the modern music of Arnold Schoenberg and Gustav Mahler in concerts. Mitropoulos died in 1960.

MONTEUX—MONTGOMERY—MOORE

Pierre Monteux   **Wes Montgomery**   **Grace Moore**

Monteux, Pierre. Known for conducting more than sixty orchestras in Europe and America and for introducing the controversial works of new composers, Pierre Monteux rebuilt and conducted the Boston Symphony Orchestra (1919-1924) and the San Francisco Symphony Orchestra (1935-1942). Born in Paris in 1875, Monteux organized his own orchestra in 1911 and drew the attention of Serge Diaghilev of the Ballet Russe. Joining the Ballet Russe, Monteux conducted the premiere of Stravinsky's *Sacre du printemps* in 1913 which brought on howls and catcalls from the audience. After serving in the French army during World War I, Monteux was invited to conduct the Boston Symphony Orchestra in 1919. He introduced the works of modern composers and became permanent conductor of the symphony. Monteux became a U.S. citizen in 1942. He died in 1964.

Montgomery, Wes. Performing in an unusual style that featured single-string fingering mixed with chord action, guitarist Wes Montgomery became a leading U.S. musician in the mid-1900s. Born in Indianapolis in 1925, Montgomery was self-taught and never learned to read music. He came to public notice in 1948 when he played with Lionel Hampton and made several records with Sonny Parker, including *Pretty Baby* and *Hamp's Gumbo*. In 1959 he joined the Mastersounds and teamed with brothers Monk and Buddy until 1960. After joining the Wynton Kelly Trio, Montgomery performed in night clubs and concerts during 1965-66. Nominated for two Grammy awards in 1965, he was voted the top jazz guitarist in a national magazine's poll of musicians. He was featured in the album *The Montgomery Brothers* and *A Day in the Life*. Montgomery died in 1968.

Moore, Grace. After a long struggle to gain a position of prominence as an opera singer, Grace Moore was featured in 1934 in *One Night of Love,* a motion picture that stimulated an interest in opera all over the world. Born in Tennessee in 1898, Miss Moore showed singing ability early in her life. She was influenced by others to become a professional singer, but when her father forbade it, Miss Moore ran away to New York, where she studied and sang in musical comedies. She was featured in Irving Berlin's Music Box Revues of 1923 and 1924. Twice she tried out for the Metropolitan Opera but failed. After studying in France she finally made her debut at the Metropolitan in 1928. Her feature role in the film *One Night of Love* brought her worldwide fame in a career that included opera, concerts, radio, and films. Miss Moore was killed in an airplane crash in 1947.

Jelly Roll Morton

Emma Nevada

Morton, Jelly Roll (Ferdinand). The first jazz composer to write his musical compositions so that the same musical arrangements could be replayed, black pianist Jelly Roll Morton claimed he invented jazz in 1901 with his "New Orleans Blues." His "Jelly Roll Blues" (1915) was the first jazz music to be published in America. Born in New Orleans in 1884, Morton played guitar as a child and later sang with a strolling quartet of gospel singers. Forming his own jazz group—Morton's Red Hot Peppers—in 1926, he performed with many jazz musicians and made a series of recordings which were later regarded as classics by critics. When jazz styles changed in the 1930s, Morton's blend of ragtime, blues, and brass band had become outdated. In 1938 Morton recorded his version of the history of jazz for the Library of Congess's Archives of American Folksong. Morton died in Los Angeles in 1941.

Nevada, Emma. Born in a California gold-mining town and brought up among miners, Emma Nevada rose to become an outstanding opera soprano and the favorite of European kings and queens in the late 19th century. Recognized as a natural coloratura with an attractive manner, Miss Nevada sang in operas all over Europe. In 1884 composer Alexander Mackenzie included a role especially for her in his *Rose of Sharon* oratorio.

Born Emma Wixom in 1859 in Alpha in the California Gold Rush country, she first sang in public at the age of 3 and two years later was showered with gold pieces when she sang to miners in Virginia City, Nevada. After attending college in Oakland, California, she went to Europe to study voice for three years before making her formal debut in a London opera under the stage name of Emma Nevada. In 1885 she married Dr. Raymond Spooner Palmer, an English doctor who became her manager. After news of her popularity reached America, she returned several times to make tours of the U.S. In England she gave performances for Queen Victoria and Edward VII, and in Spain she sang in the chambers of Christina, the queen, while her own small daughter played with the prince. Among her close friends in Europe was actress Sarah Bernhardt. Emma Nevada's voice, which had an exceptionally clear quality and extended to F above high C, began to fail in 1919, and she retired to teach voice technique. During her last years, she lived at the English home of her daughter Mignon. Emma Nevada died in 1940.

OLIVER—PAOLI—PARKER

King Oliver   **Antonio Paoli**   **Charlie Parker**

Oliver, King (Joseph). A cornet player and bandleader in New Orleans in the early 1900s, King Oliver moved to Chicago in 1918 where he organized the Creole Jazz Band and rose to become one of the most influential musicians of the jazz movement. His band recordings were among the first made by all-black groups, and they were studied by other jazz musicians, black and white, many of whom came to Chicago's South Side to hear Oliver in person.

Paoli, Antonio. Known as the Tenor of Kings and the King of Tenors, Puerto Rican-born Antonio Paoli sang before the emperor of Austria-Hungary in 1910 and was awarded the post of court singer. Born in Puerto Rico in 1872, Paoli was sent to Spain to complete his schooling. In Spain his singing attracted the attention of Princess Isabel, who persuaded the queen to sponsor his musical training. After further studies at the La Scala Singing Academy in Italy, Paoli made his debut in the opera *William Tell* in Paris. He sang in the 1900 London opera season and toured the capitals of Europe. Paoli went to New York during World War I, but was refused singing roles at the Metropolitan Opera because of the opposition of rival tenor Enrico Caruso. Paoli entered the boxing ring to earn funds to return to Europe. In 1922 he returned to Puerto Rico. Paoli died in 1946.

Born in 1885, young Oliver was playing cornet in a New Orleans brass band by 1899. In 1915 he organized his own band, and he hired his former student Louis Armstrong to play trumpet. After Oliver went to Chicago, he sent for Armstrong to join him, and both musicians helped make Chicago the new jazz capital in 1920. In later years Oliver's fame declined when other music replaced jazz in popularity. Oliver died in 1938.

Parker, Charlie. Considered one of the outstanding alto saxophonists of the 20th century, musician Charlie Parker helped create the "bop" progressive jazz movement of the 1940s that influenced later jazz musicians for decades. Born in Kansas City in 1920, Parker was playing professionally at the age of 17. A featured saxophonist with outstanding bands, including Earl "Fatha" Hines and the Billy Eckstine group, Parker introduced melodies, harmonies, tones, and rhythms in his bop solos that made him a legend in his times. He was known by the nickname Bird. Parker's solos in "Hot House" and "Salt Peanuts," which he recorded with Dizzy Gillespie in 1945, are classics. Parker formed a quintet in 1947 with Miles Davis, Max Roach, and others, and the group's recordings were reissued many times. He made his final concert appearance in New York, shortly before his death in 1955.

PORTER—RODRIGUEZ—RODZINSKI

Cole Porter — Tito Rodriguez — Artur Rodzinski

Porter, Cole. Composer of more than 100 popular songs and writer of lyrics and music for more than 40 stage and screen productions, Cole Porter contributed to many forms of musical entertainment in the mid-1900s. Born in 1893 in Indiana, Porter began his musical career in 1916 but did not become successful until 1928, when he contributed five songs to the musical *Paris*. His later stage productions included *The Gay Divorcee* (1932), *Anything Goes* (1934), *Kiss Me Kate* (1948), *Can-Can* (1953), and *Silk Stockings* (1955). Many of his plays were made into successful motion pictures. He also wrote the music for the films *High Society*, *Les Girls*, and *Rosalie*. Porter's popular songs include "Night and Day," "Begin the Beguine," "What is This Thing Called Love?," and "In the Still of the Night." Some of Porter's lyrics are witty; others are sensitive expressions of love. Porter died in 1964.

Rodriguez, Tito. Singing in a unique, rhythmic beat that represented authentic Latin style, Puerto Rican bandleader Tito Rodriguez successfully defended the traditional Latin-American love songs and dance music in the 1960s against the rising musical tide of Latin-American rock music called salsa. Born in San Juan in 1923, the only one of thirteen children to follow his father's musical career, Rodriguez sang on the radio at the age of 13 and signed his first record contract at the age of 16. In the 1940s he sang with several popular bands and in 1947 formed his own band. His group played throughout the United States and Latin America. His numerous records became popular all over America and sold more than 12 million copies. The vice-president of Argentina once thanked him for "bringing love songs back to us—people are dancing together again instead of separately." Rodriguez died in 1973.

Rodzinski, Artur. Although trained as a lawyer in his native Poland, Artur Rodzinski changed to a career in music and after World War I immigrated to the U.S., where he became a conductor and music director of many outstanding symphony orchestras. Born in Dalmatia (later part of Yugoslavia) in 1894, Rodzinski received a law degree from the University of Vienna, but gave up his practice to study conducting, piano, and composition. After service in the Austrian army in World War I, he conducted operas in Warsaw. Conductor Leopold Stokowski of the Philadelphia Symphony saw his performance in 1925 and invited Rodzinski to visit the U.S. After three years as Stokowski's assistant, Rodzinski became conductor of the Los Angeles Philharmonic, moving to the Cleveland Symphony in 1933, the New York Philharmonic in 1943, and the Chicago Symphony in 1947. He died in 1958.

Yossele Rosenblatt   **Lillian Russell**   **Olga Samaroff**

Rosenblatt, Yossele. A Jewish cantor, acclaimed throughout Europe and America in the 1920s for the quality of his tenor voice, Yossele Rosenblatt significantly influenced synagogue music as a composer of religious melodies and as a concert artist. He sang for the sound track of the first full-length sound film, *The Jazz Singer*, in 1928. Born in Russia in 1882, Rosenblatt traveled throughout Eastern Europe as a child, helping his father conduct synagogue services. He received his first appointment as a cantor at the age of 18. Moving to America in 1912, he became cantor of the Ohab Zedek Congregation in New York. Thrilling his listeners with his controlled, expressive voice that had a range of two and a half octaves, Rosenblatt became immensely popular, making many records that were reissued several times after his death. He died in 1933 while working on the film *The Dream of My People*.

Russell, Lillian. An internationally known beauty with a pleasant singing voice, Lillian Russell won great popularity as a comic opera singer in London and New York in the 1890s. She was also celebrated for her colorful personal life. Born Helen Louise Leonard in 1861 in Iowa, she was educated in a convent and later studied to be an opera singer. She made her first stage appearance in New York in 1879 in Gilbert and Sullivan's *H.M.S. Pinafore*. In 1880 she began to sing at Tony Pastor's New York Bowery Theater under the stage name of Lillian Russell. In 1899 she joined the vaudeville company of Weber and Fields, where she remained for several seasons. In the early 1900s she also played straight dramatic roles. After her fourth marriage in 1912, Miss Russell retired from the stage. She wrote beauty articles for the newspapers, lectured, and campaigned for the Red Cross. She died in 1922.

Samaroff, Olga. After years of practice in Paris and Berlin as a pianist, Olga Samaroff returned to the United States in 1905 to become one of the outstanding musical artists through her concert engagements with leading symphony orchestras and concerts. Knowing the difficulties of her own early introduction to American concert audiences, she established a charitable foundation to pay for the debuts of talented young singers and musicians. Born Lucie Hickenlooper in Texas in 1882, she studied in Europe and later changed her name to Olga Samaroff. Her family arranged to pay the cost of her first concert with the New York Symphony at Carnegie Hall in 1905, and her performance brought her numerous engagements with leading American orchestras. She married concert conductor Leopold Stokowski in 1911 and in 1925 became an instructor of piano at the Juilliard Graduate School of Music in New York. She died in 1948.

SANROMA—SCHELLING—SCHIPA

Jesus Sanroma **Ernest Schelling** **Tito Schipa**

Sanroma, Jesus Maria. An oustanding pianist whose musical education in the U.S. was financed by the Puerto Rican government, Jesus Sanroma was official pianist with the Boston Symphony Orchestra from 1926 until 1944. He was the first pianist to perform new works by several prominent 20th century composers. After he performed Stravinsky's *Capriccio*, critics said the audience went wild with enthusiasm. Sanroma gave concerts throughout the U.S., Canada, South America, and Europe, and taught at the New England Conservatory. Sanroma was born in Puerto Rico in 1903 and was sent to the U.S. at age 14 by his government to study with Antoinette Szumowska. After winning the Mason & Hamlin piano prize, he studied with Alfred Cortot in Paris and with Arthur Schnabel in Berlin. Sanroma was named chairman of the music department at the University of Puerto Rico in 1951.

Schelling, Ernest Henry. Acclaimed as an outstanding pianist, composer, and conductor, Ernest ("Uncle Ernest") Schelling introduced thousands of American youngsters to classical music in the 1920s and 30s. He started the New York Philharmonic Symphony Society's Young People's Concerts in 1924, appearing in that weekly series for fifteen years, and conducted children's orchestral concerts all over the United States. Born in New Jersey in 1876, Schelling was a child prodigy who made his first appearance as a concert pianist at age 4. After studying in Europe for several years, he joined the Boston Symphony Orchestra in 1905 and became a well-known concert artist in America. After injuring his hands in an automobile accident in 1919, Schelling devoted much of his time to composing. His most famous composition was *A Victory Ball* (1925). Schelling died in New York City in 1939.

Schipa, Tito. An operatic tenor whose career spanned the years 1911-59, Tito Schipa entertained audiences with his gifted lyric style and was regarded by music critics as one of the foremost opera singers of the first half of the 1900s. Born Raffaele Amedeo in Italy in 1889, Schipa began his musical career as a composer and started singing at 15, making his operatic debut in 1911. He sang at La Scala Opera in Italy in 1915 in *Prince Igor*. His first American appearance was in 1919 at the Chicago Civic Opera, where he remained until 1932. He made his New York debut in 1932 at the Metropolitan Opera and later sang leading roles in many popular operas, including *La Traviata*, *Lucia*, and *Don Giovanni*. A special favorite in his Russian and South America tours, Schipa was still in demand as a concert singer at age 70. Composer of the operetta *Principessa Liana* and church music, Schipa died in 1965.

SCHOENBERG—SCHUYLER

Arnold Schoenberg

Schoenberg, Arnold. Although he wrote music in a style that was difficult to play and to appreciate, composer Arnold Schoenberg was acclaimed as one of the 20th century's music masters. Born in Austria in 1874, Schoenberg at eight began studying the violin and at nine was composing music for it. Unable to afford music lessons, he was almost entirely self-taught. His earliest works followed the popular styles of that day, but his first successful composition was the 1899 tone poem *Verklaerte Nacht* (Transfigured Night), a sextet for strings. It was the most popular of all Schoenberg's compositions and later became the music for the ballet *Pillar of Fire*. He wrote a symphonic poem, *Pelleas and Melisande*, in 1902 and in 1911 produced a huge choral composition, *Gurrelieder* (The Songs of Gurre).

Schoenberg next began experimenting with musical composition; but his music, no longer played in one key, was displeasing to most listeners. He was disappointed and gave up composing for the next seven years, working instead on a method of organizing tone. He introduced a new theory in 1921, referring to it as a "Method of Composing with Twelve Tones." He soon discovered that audiences were more interested in his system than in listening to his music. Schoenberg came to America in 1933 and taught first at the University of Southern California and later at the University of California at Los Angeles. In 1922 he completed the first two acts of a biblical opera, *Moses and Aaron*, which were performed many times before his death in 1951.

Philippa Schuyler

Schuyler, Philippa. Astounding the musical world with her exceptional talents as a child, black pianist and composer Philippa Schuyler played the piano at two and her first symphonic composition, "Manhattan Nocturne," was performed at Carnegie Hall when she was 13. Born in 1932 in New York City, Miss Schuyler was taught almost as an infant to read and write. When tested by amazed educators, she was found to have an I.Q. of 185. By the time she was four, she had composed ten pieces and, at five, gave her first public recital in Newark's Fuld Hall. At 12 she won the first and second prizes in a competition for young composers and traveled to Detroit to hear the Detroit Symphony Orchestra play one of her compositions.

Miss Schuyler made her concert soloist debut at 12, playing Saint-Saens's *Second Piano Concerto* with the New York Philharmonic orchestra. She was just 14 when her composition "Rumpelstiltskin" was performed by the Boston Pops Orchestra, with herself as guest soloist. Later, the composition was played by the Dixon Youth Orchestra, the New Haven Symphony Orchestra, and the New York Philharmonic. Acclaimed by music critics, she was in demand everywhere. At the request of the U.S. State Department, she made good-will tours of more than 50 countries. After returning from a 1959 world tour, she made her first Carnegie Hall recital at a benefit performance before the season's largest audience for classical music. She wrote of her tour experiences in *Adventures in Black and White* and authored *Who Killed the Congo*. Miss Schuyler died in the late 1960s.

Bessie Smith

Albert Spalding

Smith, Bessie. Hailed as the Empress of the Blues, Bessie Smith helped make blues a recognized American art form, as well as an outlet for the sorrows of black people in the 1920s. Her popularity as a singer grew to such heights that a new Bessie Smith record was considered a public event in Chicago, and people lined up for blocks to buy a copy. She made 80 records between 1924 and 1927 that sold more than six million copies. Many of her accompanists, including Louis Armstrong and Fletcher Henderson, later became outstanding musicians in their own right, and critics believed that her earthy style of singing influenced American music for decades.

Bessie Smith was born in Chattanooga, Tennessee in 1894 and was singing publicly at the age of nine. She toured the South during the early 1920s, singing in carnivals and tent shows. Columbia recording director Frank Walker signed her to record "Down Hearted Blues" after hearing her sing in Alabama, and the record sold more than 2 million copies in 1923. She continued to be widely popular until the end of the 1920s, when changing fashions and publicity about her personal problems began to affect her popularity, and the approach of the economic depression of the 30s threatened the entire recording industry. Bessie Smith bled to death from injuries received in an automobile accident in 1937, after a hospital in Mississippi refused to admit her for treatment. Edward Albee, the noted playwright, dramatized the circumstances of her death in his play, *The Death of Bessie Smith*.

Spalding, Albert. An outstanding violinist whose playing was praised by music critics throughout the world, Albert Spalding was the only American violinist asked to perform at the La Scala opera house in Milan, Italy. He was also the only American violinist ever invited to appear as a soloist with the Paris Conservatory Orchestra. Born in Chicago in 1888, Spalding graduated from the Bologna Conservatory in Italy at age 14, receiving the highest honors of any musician since Mozart. He performed his first concert at age 16 in Paris and made his first American appearance at Carnegie Hall in 1908 with the New York Symphony Society. Enlisting in the air force at the outbreak of World War I, Spalding was decorated by the governments of Italy and France. Resuming his musical career after the war, he toured the U.S. and Europe and composed more than sixty works for the violin. Spalding died in 1953.

STOKOWSKI—STRAVINSKY

Leopold Stokowski

Stokowski, Leopold. Encouraging the performance of controversial contemporary music and working for the most faithful interpretation of all classical music, Leopold Stokowski conducted many of America's outstanding symphony orchestras during the first half of the 20th century. Introducing the work of eminent European composers, including Stravinsky, Schoenberg, and Prokofiev, to American audiences, he also conducted the first performances of significant works by American composers, including Aaron Copland and Ernest Schelling. Through his intensive study of acoustics and his insistence upon the most satisfactory recording conditions, Stokowski improved the methods used to record music in the United States.

Stokowski was born in London in 1882 and studied music at the Royal College of Music in London and the Paris Conservatory. He accepted a position as organist at St. Bartholomew's Church in New York in 1905, and became conductor of the Cincinnati Symphony Orchestra in 1909. He was named conductor of the Philadelphia Symphony in 1912 and developed it so effectively that he was given the Bok Award. The first conductor to employ young as well as female musicians, Stokowski organized the All-American Youth Orchestra in 1940 and gave concerts throughout the world. Stokowski appeared in several movies, including Walt Disney's *Fantasia* in 1941. He also conducted the NBC Symphony Orchestra, the Hollywood Bowl Symphony, the New York Philharmonic, and the Houston Symphony, and formed the American Symphony Orchestra in New York in 1962.

Igor Stravinsky

Stravinsky, Igor F. When Igor Stravinsky's ballet *The Rites of Spring* was first performed in Paris in 1913, the audience was so enraged by the wild, unfamiliar music, that they started a riot. But only ten years later, *Rites* was considered an outstanding musical composition, and Stravinsky was recognized as one of the most influential composers of the 20th century. Combining harmonies in two different keys with complicated rhythmic patterns, Stravinsky created music unlike any that had been heard before, featuring new sounds and tempos in his ballets, symphonies, and concerts.

Stravinsky was born in Russia in 1882 and graduated from law school in 1905. Instead of practicing law, he decided to study music with composer Rimsky-Korsakov and worked closely with him until the composer's death in 1908. Commissioned by Sergei Diaghilev to compose scores for the Ballet Russe, Stravinsky wrote *The Firebird* (1910), *Petrouchka* (1911), and *The Rites of Spring* (1913). The three compositions firmly established his reputation as an outstanding composer. After losing his home and property during the Russian Revolution, Stravinsky moved first to Switzerland and then to France. The music he composed while living in France is generally considered more conventional than his early ballets. Stravinsky immigrated to the U.S. during World War II and became a citizen in 1945. He composed many significant works, including the jazz-inspired ballet *Orpheus* (1947), and several compositions using Arnold Schoenberg's 12-tone scale. Stravinsky died in 1971.

Gustav Strube

Gladys Swarthout

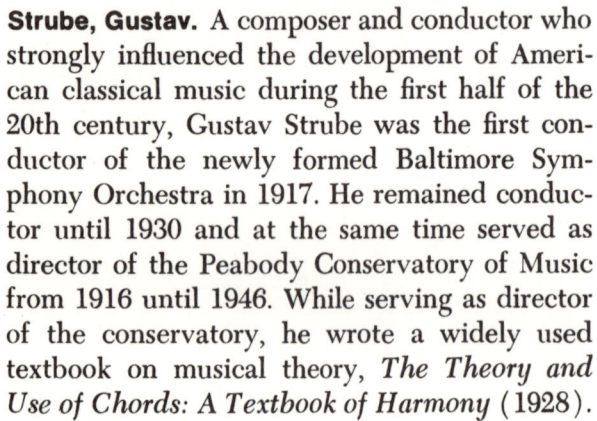

Strube, Gustav. A composer and conductor who strongly influenced the development of American classical music during the first half of the 20th century, Gustav Strube was the first conductor of the newly formed Baltimore Symphony Orchestra in 1917. He remained conductor until 1930 and at the same time served as director of the Peabody Conservatory of Music from 1916 until 1946. While serving as director of the conservatory, he wrote a widely used textbook on musical theory, *The Theory and Use of Chords: A Textbook of Harmony* (1928).

Strube was born in Bellenstedt, Germany in 1867 and was taught to play the violin by his father. He studied at the Leipzig Conservatory with Adolph Brodsky, an internationally recognized teacher. Later, he became a member of the Gewandhaus Orchestra in Leipzig. Immigrating to the United States in 1891, Strube accepted a position as violinist with the Boston Symphony Orchestra and remained for twenty-two years. He was appointed chairman of the musical theory department at the Peabody Conservatory in Baltimore in 1913 and three years later was selected as conductor of the Baltimore Symphony. During his years in Baltimore, Strube composed many musical works with uniquely American themes, including three symphonies, three overtures, two violin concertos, and several other compositions that were highly praised by music critics. They include: *Lanier* (1925), dedicated to the American musician, Sidney Lanier; *Americana* (1930); and *Peace Overture* (1945). He also composed two operas, *Ramona* and *The Captive*. Strube died in 1953.

Swarthout, Gladys. Acclaimed both for her outstanding mezzo soprano voice and her dramatic talent as an actress, Gladys Swarthout sang from 1929 until 1945 with the Metropolitan Opera, where her portrayal of Carmen was especially popular with New York audiences. She also appeared on radio and in several motion pictures. Born in Missouri in 1904, Miss Swarthout decided at age seven that she wanted to become a singer. After studying at Chicago's Bush Conservatory of Music for three years, she performed with the Chicago Civic Opera Company and the Ravinia Opera Company before joining the Metropolitan in 1929. She later appeared in several films, including *Give Us This Night* (1936), *Champagne Waltz* (1937), and *Romance in the Dark* (1938). She included musical comedy tunes as well as classics in her many concerts. Miss Swarthout died in Italy in 1969.

SZELL—TATUM—TAYLOR

George Szell   **Art Tatum**   **Deems Taylor**

Szell, George. Starting as a talented child pianist, George Szell studied music and began his long career as a conductor at age 17 when he was selected to conduct the Vienna Symphony Orchestra in 1914. Szell was so well accepted that he chose conducting as his new career. By 1940 he was regarded one of the most respected conductors in the world. In 1946 he was appointed conductor of the Cleveland Orchestra, a post he held for the remainder of his life. Born in Hungary in 1897, Szell left school at seven to study piano. After his appearance with the Vienna Symphony, he joined the Berlin State Opera, eventually becoming chief conductor. Szell first appeared in America in 1930 with the St. Louis Symphony. From 1942 to 1946, he conducted the New York Metropolitan Opera Orchestra. The Cleveland Orchestra grew to international prominence under Szell's leadership. He died in 1970.

Tatum, Art (Arthur). Almost totally blind from birth, Art Tatum became one of America's leading pianists in the mid-1900s by blending a classical style of music with jazz. His technical ability was so unique that other musicians considered his style too classical to be regarded as jazz. Born in Ohio in 1910, Tatum attended the Cousino School for the Blind in Columbus and studied for two years at the Toledo School of Music. He formed his own band in 1926 and later performed as a solo pianist in Cleveland nightclubs. In 1932 he became popular as accompanist for singer Adelaide Hall in New York, and he later was a favorite in Chicago and New York nightclubs. Tatum made appearances in England in 1938 and began annual concert tours in 1945. During the early 1950s, he made many recordings. His 1956 concert appearance at the Hollywood Bowl attracted more than 19,000 people. Tatum died later that year.

Taylor, (Joseph) Deems. A composer in his own right of significant choral works and operas, Deems Taylor became known throughout the U.S. during the mid-1900s as a radio commentator on classical music performed by symphony orchestras. His nationwide radio talks explaining broadcasts of the New York Philharmonic Society popularized symphonic music. Born in 1885 in New York, Taylor graduated in 1906 from New York University. Deciding to follow a double career as journalist and composer, he joined the editorial staff of the *New York Tribune* and later became an associate editor of *Collier's Weekly*. Taylor's first success as a composer was a prize-winning tone poem, *The Siren Song* (1913). With *The King's Henchman* (1927) and *Peter Ibbetson* (1931), he became the first native-born American composer to have two operas presented at the Metropolitan Opera. Taylor died in 1966.

TIBBETT—TRAUBEL—VARESE

Lawrence Tibbett　　**Helen Traubel**　　**Edgar Varese**

Tibbett, Lawrence M. Appearing with the Metropolitan Opera Company from 1923 to 1950, Lawrence Tibbett was one of the first American opera singers to prove that formal voice training in Europe was not a requirement for becoming an outstanding operatic baritone. Hired as an understudy at the Metropolitan, Tibbett achieved overnight success when he replaced the regular performer in a major role in *Falstaff.* He was rewarded with a "standing ovation."

Traubel, Helen. The first American-born and trained soprano to become a leading interpreter of German operatic roles at the Metropolitan Opera, Helen Traubel in the mid-1900s added to her popularity by appearing in nightclubs and motion pictures and on television. Born in St. Louis in 1903, Miss Traubel left high school to study voice and made her professional debut in a few years with the St. Louis Symphony Orchestra. In 1937 she appeared in her first operatic role at the Metropolitan in a performance of Damrosch's *The Man Without a Country.* Her first Wagnerian opera role was in a 1939 Chicago production of *Die Walküre.* In later appearances at the Metropolitan Opera, she sang leading roles in many other operas, including *Lohengrin* and *Der Rosenkavalier.* When her appearances in nightclubs met with disapproval from Metropolitan officials in 1953, Miss Traubel left the Metropolitan. She died in 1972.

During the next two decades, Tibbett sang the major baritone roles in many French and Italian operas and was the first to sing the leading baritone role in several American operas, including *The Emperor Jones.* Born in Bakersfield, California in 1896, Tibbett began singing in movie theaters and church choirs after graduating from high school. He helped found the American Guild of Musical Artists in 1936. Tibbett died in New York in 1960.

Varèse, Edgar. A composer whose musical experiments created considerable controversy in the mid-1900s, Edgar Varèse wrote orchestral music that featured percussion sounds rather than melody or harmony. Born in Paris in 1885, Varèse studied composition there, then moved to Berlin, where he lived until 1914. During World War I, all the music he had written was destroyed. Varèse immigrated to America in 1915 and settled in New York, where he organized concerts for music that stressed unusual sound effects and complex rhythms. He founded the New York Symphony Orchestra in 1919 and the International Composers' Guild in 1921. His *Ionisation* was composed for two groups of percussion players, thirteen in all, using an imprecise pitch. His *Equatorial* used brass, organ, percussion, and electronic music. In 1958 he coproduced *Poème Electronique* for the Brussels Exhibition. Varèse died in 1965.

WALLER—WALTER—WHITE, Clarence

Fats Waller **Bruno Walter** **Clarence White**

Waller, Fats (Thomas). A Baptist minister's son who studied piano and organ, Fats Waller became a celebrated jazz musician and composer of the 1920s and 30s. His entertaining talk on stage and exciting piano style made him popular in the U.S. He composed many jazz songs, including "Ain't Misbehavin'" and "Honeysuckle Rose." Born in the Harlem section of New York City in 1904, Waller at ten was playing piano at school concerts and organ in his father's church. He learned quickly to play syncopated jazz piano from James P. Johnson, and together they entertained at parties and in night clubs. Waller and Johnson wrote the music for a Broadway show, *Keep Shufflin'*, in 1928, and in 1929 Waller wrote the music for the *Hot Chocolate* revue. Waller toured Europe several times in the 1930s and in 1932 gave an organ recital in Notre Dame Cathedral in Paris. He died in New York in 1943.

Walter, Bruno. One of Europe's outstanding conductors, Bruno Walter fled to America when Adolf Hitler came to power in Germany, and he served as conductor and musical adviser for the New York Philharmonic from 1947 to 1949. Born Bruno Walter Schlesinger in Berlin in 1876, Walter studied at the Stern Conservatory and at 17 was voice coach at the Cologne Opera. In 1894 he became assistant conductor under Gustav Mahler at the Municipal Theater in Hamburg. Appointed general director of the Munich Opera in 1917, Walter made it one of Europe's finest. Walter made his American debut as a guest conductor in 1922 and was appointed conductor of the Salzburg Mozart Festival the same year. In 1932-35 he served under Arturo Toscanini at the New York Philharmonic, and in 1936 he became music director of the Vienna Opera. Walter also wrote *Theme and Variations* (1947). He died in 1962.

White, Clarence C. For his writing of the opera *Ouanga*, based on the life of the Haitian liberator Dessalines, Clarence White was awarded the David Bispham Medal, an annual award given for the most significant operatic composition of the year. Born in 1880 in Tennessee, White moved to Washington, D.C. with his parents. After attending Howard University, he entered the Oberlin College Conservatory, where he played first violin in the orchestra. After graduation he traveled to London for further study and became a pupil of Russian violinist Zacharewitsch in 1908. White became first violinist in the Croydon (England) String Players' Club and returned to Boston in 1910 to open a private studio. He won international recognition for his music in the early 1900s. Appointed music director at West Virginia State College in 1924, White wrote *Ouanga* with James F. Mathews. White died in 1960.

WHITE, Josh—WHITEMAN—YOUNG

Josh White **Paul Whiteman** **Lester Young**

White, Josh. Traveling around the country helping blind musicians as a boy in the 1920s, Josh White learned to sing and play the guitar and became a popular folk singer. He also composed ballads about the hardships of blacks in a white society. Born in South Carolina in 1915, the son of a minister, White was seven when he began accompanying a blind singer. For the next ten years, White took care of blind musicians traveling from city to city. He soon began to sing and play the guitar himself, making his first recording at age 11. Known as the Singing Christian, he joined a radio group, the Southernaires, in the 1930s. When a hand injury kept him from playing the guitar, White worked as an elevator operator. In 1940 he appeared on Broadway with Paul Robeson in the musical *John Henry*. Two of his most popular albums of folk songs are *Chain Gang* and *Southern Exposure*. White died in 1969.

Whiteman, Paul. Originator of a smooth style of dance rhythms based on a mixture of jazz and concert music, orchestra leader Paul Whiteman became popular as The King of Jazz during the 1920s. Born in Denver in 1891, Whiteman was a skillful musician and arranger. Realizing the commercial value of popular music influenced by jazz, Whiteman encouraged George Gershwin's symphonic jazz experiments and introduced Gershwin's *Rhapsody in Blue* at a New York concert in 1924. He also encouraged Ferde Grofe in his production of musical works. Whiteman's band included jazz greats Bix Beiderbecke, Red Norvo, and Jack Teagarden. He introduced many song hits, including "Whispering," "Avalon," and "Song of India." His popularity waned during the 1930s, and he broke up his band. He became a disk jockey and later served successfully as musical director of a radio network. Whiteman died in 1967.

Young, Lester. Rated by critics of jazz music as a leading saxophonist and teacher of the 1930s and 1940s, Lester Young exerted a lasting influence on American jazz through musicians who followed his techniques and through his many recordings. Born into a musical family in 1909, Young grew up playing at carnivals with the family band, but quit when faced with "Jim Crow" restrictions on blacks in the South. A master of several instruments, he began to concentrate on the tenor saxophone and by the early 1930s played with leading bands, including those of Count Basie and Fletcher Henderson. With Basie he acquired the nickname "Prez," short for president, a title conferred on him by singer Billie Holliday. He served in the army in 1944-45 and after his discharge joined Norman Granz's "Jazz at the Philharmonic" show. He made several trips overseas in the 1950s. Young died in 1959.

ANDERSON—BACHARACH

Marian Anderson

Burt Bacharach

Anderson, Marian. The first black singer to appear at New York City's Metropolitan Opera (1955), Marian Anderson, singing the leading role of Ulrica in *Masked Ball*, was acclaimed as having one of the finest contralto voices in America. Born in 1902 in Philadelphia, she sang as a child in the choir of the Union Baptist Church, where the pure quality and wide range of her voice were first recognized. Unable to afford singing lessons at 19 years of age, her church paid for a year's study with famous teacher Giuseppe Boghetti. Impressed with her talent, Boghetti gave her a scholarship for her second year of training. In 1925 she won a concert tour that included an appearance with the New York Philharmonic Orchestra. Her performance in her first solo concert at New York's Town Hall in 1935 was a great success. One critic remarked that her "music-making probes too deep for words."

Miss Anderson, finding many concert stages closed to her in America because of her race, went abroad to study and perform. In 1939 she was barred from singing at an Easter Sunday concert at Constitution Hall in Washington, D.C. by the owners, the Daughters of the American Revolution. In a strong protest, Eleanor Roosevelt announced her resignation from the D.A.R. and helped arrange an appearance for Miss Anderson on the steps of the Lincoln Memorial, where she sang for 75,000 people. After concert tours in Europe, the Orient, and India sponsored by the U.S. State Department, Miss Anderson was appointed a U.S. delegate to the United Nations in 1958.

Bacharach, Burt. Winner of a 1970 Academy Award for music and composer of a popular Broadway musical, Burt Bacharach created a refreshing style of music that appealed to both young and old audiences during the 1960s and 70s. Described as a combination of rock, Latin, and gospel styles, Bacharach's music, with its unusual rhythms, was accepted as a new sound. Born in 1929, Bacharach studied at McGill University. After serving in the army, he formed an association with songwriter Hal David. The team attracted the attention of leading singers and motion picture and theatrical producers. Popular recordings of Bacharach's songs include "Walk on By," "Reach Out for Me," and "Do You Know the Way to San Jose?". Bacharach later composed the score of the Broadway musical *Promises, Promises* (1968). He won the Academy Award for his music in *Butch Cassidy and The Sundance Kid* (1970).

BAILEY—BAKER—BALLARD

Pearl Bailey   **Josephine Baker**   **Louis W. Ballard**

Bailey, Pearl. Her relaxed style, quick wit, and friendliness with audiences made Pearl Bailey one of America's most popular singers and entertainers beginning in the 1930s. After performing in nightclubs, on stage and radio, Miss Bailey had her own show on national television in 1971. Born in Virginia in 1918, she moved to Philadelphia in 1933 and sang professionally in clubs throughout Pennsylvania. She joined the Cootie Williams and Count Basie bands as a singer, and after engagements in New York, she toured with the U.S.O. during World War II. Miss Bailey won the Donaldson Award for her stage debut in *St. Louis Woman* (1946), appeared in the movie *Carmen Jones* (1954), and starred in the Broadway musical *House of Flowers* (1954). One of her most popular performances was her award-winning role with Cab Calloway in the all-black Broadway presentation of *Hello Dolly*, which opened in 1967.

Baker, Josephine. After attracting attention as a singer and dancer in America during the 1920s, Josephine Baker achieved international fame as a club entertainer at the Folies-Bergere in Paris. Born in St. Louis in 1906, Miss Baker lived in poverty in a one-room house. When 15 she scraped together enough money to hear blues singer Bessie Smith, a noted black entertainer, perform in St. Louis. That night, she left home as Miss Smith's maid. Within a few months, Miss Baker was dancing in the chorus line of the musical *Shuffle Along* in New York City. She won small parts on Broadway and, in 1925, traveled to Paris with the *Revue Negre*. Miss Baker's jazz style quickly became popular, and she was featured as a main attraction at the Folies-Bergere. During World War II, she served as a nurse with the Free French Army. After marrying, she retired in 1956 in France, adopting 11 children. She died in 1975.

Ballard, Louis W. Composer of music with themes based on Indian legends, Louis Ballard was nominated for the 1972 Pulitzer Prize in music for his innovative composition *Desert Trilogy*. Born in 1931 in Oklahoma, Ballard, a Quapaw Cherokee, graduated from Tulsa University in 1953. Awarded an F. B. Parriott Graduate Fellowship in 1961, Ballard returned to Tulsa University to receive his master's degree. As consultant for the Bureau of Indian Affairs schools, Ballard designed programs of studies in Indian music, stressing the instruments and background of Indian musical sources. In the 1960s he established the first all-Indian film company in America. Later Ballard became president of the Santa Fe Symphony Orchestra. His first major work, *Koshare, An American Indian Ballet,* was performed in 1966 and won wide acclaim. In 1972 Ballard composed a new cantata, *Portrait of Will Rogers.*

Count Basie

Harry Belafonte

Basie, Count (William). From the tradition of rhythm and blues music, black pianist and bandleader William "Count" Basie during the 1930s created a new and widely imitated jazz sound called the Kansas City style. Basie began his performance with a piano solo, then each member of his fifteen-man band played a variation of the solo on his own instrument. After every member had performed, the complete band played together for a closing harmony. Basie's Kansas City sound was described as "large, robust, and always swinging . . . with the light, infectious piano tinkling of its leader."

Born in 1904, Basie received music lessons from his mother and later learned to play ragtime by listening to the organist in a local movie theater. Basie began his professional career in the 1920s, touring with a vaudeville show. After the show broke up in 1927 in Kansas City, Basie earned his living by playing piano in a movie theater. The following year he joined Walter Page's Blue Devils and later played with Bennie Moten's group. After forming his own band in 1935, he was nicknamed The Count. Urged by a music critic in 1936, Basie and his band moved to New York City, performed at the Famous Door Club, and began recording. His band toured the U.S. and Europe in the 1950s and played a command performance for the Queen of England in 1957. Basie's most popular recordings include "One O'Clock Jump," "April in Paris," "Blues by Basie," and "A Night at the Apollo." Widely celebrated, even after the popularity of big bands declined, Basie continued to perform during the 1960s and 70s.

Belafonte, Harry. After popularizing the calypso ballad in the 1940s, Harry Belafonte became one of America's most celebrated folk singers and actors. Born to West Indian parents in New York in 1927, Belafonte served in the navy and worked as a janitor while attending a drama workshop. In 1949 he began singing in nightclubs as a jazz vocalist. Interested in folk music, he spent nearly two years researching folk songs and styles. In 1951 Belafonte opened at New York's Village Vanguard as a casually dressed calypso singer. His arrangements of "Matilda" and "The Banana Boat Song," and his relaxed style, which captured the mood of the Caribbean, made him popular. While recording and singing in nightclubs, Belafonte played in Broadway shows and films, starring in movies, including *Carmen Jones*, a modern version of the opera *Carmen*, *Odds Against Tomorrow*, and *Buck and the Preacher*.

BERLIN—BERNSTEIN

Irving Berlin

Berlin, Irving. For more than fifty years, Irving Berlin composed popular music which reflected the changing moods of 20th century America. Many of his songs, including "God Bless America" and "White Christmas", became American classics. Born Isidor Baline in Russia in 1888, he settled in New York City and started his career as a singing waiter in Chinatown. Although he had no formal training in music, he soon proved his gift for writing lyrics and songs. One of his first songs, "Alexander's Ragtime Band" (1911), made Berlin a celebrity, and his tune, "A Pretty Girl Is Like a Melody," became the unofficial theme song of the early Ziegfeld Follies. Drafted into the army in 1917, Berlin composed the music for the army benefit show, *Yip, Yip, Yaphank*, which included "Oh, How I Hate To Get Up In the Morning." After the war, his music for the stage play *The Coconuts*, which starred the Marx brothers, caught the carefree spirit of the 1920s.

Berlin's songs changed during the Depression. His musicals *Face the Music* and *As Thousands Cheer* reflected the problems of the 1930s. After the Depression, Berlin again composed music in a lighter style. His songs for the films *Top Hat, Easter Parade, There's No Business Like Show Business*, and *White Christmas* sold millions of records. During World War II, Berlin's production *This Is The Army* helped raise $10 million for the Army Emergency Relief Fund. In 1955 President Eisenhower awarded Berlin a gold medal for his contributions to American patriotism.

Leonard Bernstein

Bernstein, Leonard. One of the most creative and versatile men of music in the twentieth century, conductor, composer, and teacher Leonard Bernstein awakened a new musical interest in millions of Americans. His programs were fresh and unusual, appealing to audiences of many ages and tastes. Bernstein devoted whole concerts to the work of one composer or to one musical form. As a composer, he created both concert and popular music which won praise from critics, listeners, and musicians.

Born in Lawrence, Massachusetts, August 25, 1918, Bernstein chose a career in music against his family's wishes. Following his graduation from Harvard, he studied at the Curtis Institute of Music in Philadelphia. Bernstein first won national acclaim in 1951 as conductor of the Berkshire Music Festival in Tanglewood, Massachusetts. Later, he won appointment as a conductor of the New York Philharmonic orchestra. He created the music for *On The Town, Wonderful Town* and *West Side Story* and composed chamber music and the symphonies *Jeremiah, Kaddish,* and *The Age of Anxiety*. His ballet *Fancy Free*, his choral compositions including *Chichester Psalms*, and his controversial *Mass* composed for the opening of the John F. Kennedy Center for the Performing Arts in Washington, D.C., helped establish Bernstein as a major composer of the 1960s and 70s. A stimulating author and teacher, Bernstein conducted a series of Young People's Concerts, and in his book *The Joy of Music*, he outlines methods to help listeners increase their understanding and appreciation.

James Brown

John Cage

Brown, James. The talents and performing style of black singer James Brown helped soul music —a mixture of blues, rock, and gospel—become popular in the 1950s and 60s. Interested in developing black communities, Brown later invested money to help blacks buy their own businesses and often appeared at fund-raising benefit shows. Born in Georgia in 1934, Brown trained to become a boxer. He first made recordings in a Macon, Georgia radio station in 1956. Encouraged by his rising popularity, Brown devoted full time to his music and organized a troupe which toured the U.S. in 1965. Attracting large crowds, the group earned over a million dollars. Brown's most popular songs include "Please, Please, Please," "It's a Man's World," and "I Feel Good." A frequent television and recording artist, Brown performed for servicemen in Vietnam and in 1968 drew a capacity crowd at a Yankee Stadium concert.

Cage, John. Experimenting with unique sounds produced by electric buzzers, flower pots, and automobile hoods, 20th century pianist and composer John Cage created new and interesting tonal variations that attracted wide attention. Cage's first major composition *Prepared Piano* featured an ordinary piano with bolts, clothespins, and dolls' arms inserted between the strings. The result was described as a mixture of "pings, plucks, and delicate thuds." Cage defined his music as a combination of silence, sound, and rhythm and stoutly defended it by saying that although it had little relationship to harmony, it did create unusual and interesting sounds. His compositions allowed performers the choice of many musical arrangements.

Born in Los Angeles, California in 1912, Cage first studied under private tutors at Pomona College, and in Europe. Returning to the U.S. in 1936, Cage joined the Cornish School faculty. His first concert in New York in 1943 featured the collection of odd "noninstruments," including scrap metal. For creating *Prepared Piano* in 1948, Cage won an award from the National Academy of Arts and Letters and also received a Guggenheim Fellowship. Cage's later works include *Imaginary Landscape No. 4* (1951), composed for a "pianist, radio, whistle, water pail, and a deck of cards." *Water Music,* composed in 1952, featured 12 separate radios tuned to different stations. Searching for new ways to create unique sounds, Cage once remarked: "Just as you go along the beach and pick up pretty shells that please you, I go into the piano and find sounds that I like."

CALLOWAY—CAPO—CARDIN

Cab Calloway **Bobby Capo** **Fred Cardin**

Calloway, Cab (Cabell). After he rose to national fame during the 1930s as a band leader at New York's Cotton Club, Cab Calloway became an internationally popular singer, actor, songwriter, and musician. Born December 25, 1907 in New York, Calloway first appeared at the Cotton Club at 22, alternating with Duke Ellington. During the 1930s, Calloway wrote and recorded his theme song "Minnie the Moocher," and later he and his orchestra were featured in movies, including *Big Broadcast* (1932), *Stormy Weather* (1943), and *International House* (1933). Calloway disbanded his orchestra to work as a soloist with smaller groups and later began an acting career. He played the roles of Sportin' Life in the musical *Porgy and Bess* (1953) and Horace Vandergelden in the black version of *Hello Dolly* (1967). Calloway remained a popular entertainer for more than 40 years.

Capo, Bobby. One of the most widely recorded Spanish composers of the 1950s and 60s, Puerto Rican singer Bobby Capo captivated American and European audiences with his complete mastery of the Latin ballad. Born in Coamo, Puerto Rico in 1922, Capo wrote his first song at the age of 12. After achieving recognition for his singing talent in high school, Capo performed on a national radio network. While singing with a popular recording band in 1940, he developed an interest in writing his own music. Leaving the band the next year, he began his career as a soloist and musical composer. He wrote more than 1,000 songs, many of which were later recorded by international performers. His most popular titles include "Amor y Mas Amor" and "Sonando Con Puerto Rico." During the 1960s Capo hosted many television and radio programs in Puerto Rico and later in New York.

Cardin, Fred. Creating compositions for violin, chorus, and orchestra—including the music for ten historical pageants—Quapaw Indian composer Fred Cardin interpreted Indian life and traditions for 20th century Americans. He composed *Cree War Dance; Thunder Mountain*, a musical expression of Indian culture; and *Great Drum*, first performed as part of an all-American concert in New York City. Born in Oklahoma, Cardin studied violin while growing up on a reservation. He won a scholarship to the Dana Musical Institute and became first violinist with an all-Indian quartet. After serving in World War I, he played with the Kansas City Symphony Orchestra and taught violin at the University of Nebraska. He formed the Cardin-Lieurance String Quartet and later directed the Standard Symphony Orchestra. Cardin was recognized as an authority on Indian culture and music and lectured throughout the U.S.

Vikki Carr **Diahann Carroll** **Johnny Cash**

Carr, Vikki. Displaying a uniquely sensitive singing style, Mexican-American Vikki Carr brought new warmth and intimacy to her renditions of popular music in the 1960s and 70s. Born in El Paso, Texas, Miss Carr grew up in Rosemead, California. Her parents named her Florencia Bisenta de Casillas Martinez Cardona, but she later adopted the stage name of Vikki Carr. Completing high school in Rosemead, she had gained experience by appearing in school musicals. She joined the Pepe Callahan Mexican-Irish Band as a featured singer. Later she became a soloist and appeared on many television shows as well as in nightclubs. Among her recordings are "It Must Be Him," her biggest seller, and "That's All." A performer who cried when singing sad songs, she explained her feelings by repeating the lyrics of one of her popular songs: "I can give love that lasts forever, that's all."

Carroll, Diahann. Winning the 1969 title role in "Julia," the first national television situation comedy to feature a black actress, was one of many accomplishments for singer-actress-comedienne Diahann Carroll. Born Carol Diahann Johnson in New York in 1935, the daughter of a subway conductor, Miss Carroll became a fashion model at fifteen and at nineteen appeared in the Broadway musical *House of Flowers*. She played her first movie role in 1954 as Myrt in *Carmen Jones*. A featured television guest, she appeared in many serious dramas as well as a singer and comedienne on variety programs. Appearing again on Broadway in 1962 in the Richard Rogers musical *No Strings*, Miss Carroll was acclaimed by critics for her beauty and captivating singing style. Supported by outstanding musical groups, she recorded many albums that featured the most popular songs from her musicals and night club acts.

Cash, Johnny. Winning gold record awards for his million-seller albums of *Ring of Fire, I Walk the Line*, and *Johnny Cash At Folsom Prison*, Johnny Cash became one of America's most popular singers and talented composers of 20th century country and western music. A part-Cherokee Indian who was born in an Arkansas shack in 1932, Cash served in the air force from 1950 to 1954, then settled in Memphis, Tennessee, where he sold appliances. His first record *Cry, Cry, Cry* (1955) brought a recording contract, and by 1958 he had sold over six million records. Appealing to a vast audience, Cash's songs about railroad men, hoboes, and gamblers gained him recognition as a musical spokesman for young and old. He was named outstanding folk singer and composer of 1970. Cash's weekly television program featuring his home-spun qualities helped popularize country and western music.

CASSADORE—CHARLES—COLEMAN

Philip Cassadore **Ray Charles** **Ornette Coleman**

Cassadore, Philip. By teaching the cultural history of the Apache Indian through native folk songs, singer and Indian affairs consultant Philip Cassadore, beginning in the 1960s, helped promote the study of Apache culture in university anthropology departments. His songs were taken from authentic ceremonials and vividly describe the religious rituals of the Apache. Born in Arizona in 1933, Cassadore studied at Brigham Young University. Most of his songs were learned from his father Broken Arrow, an Apache chief and medicine man. With his sister Patsy, Cassadore recorded four albums of Indian folk songs. He later conducted a weekly radio program for the Apache Indians and served as an Indian affairs consultant on radio and television shows. During the 1960s and early 70s, Cassadore directed the Community Action Program at the San Carlos Reservation in Arizona.

Charles, Ray. Best known for the introduction of "soul music," black entertainer Ray Charles won acclaim as a creative singer, pianist, saxophonist, and composer in the 1960s and 70s. Charles described "soul" as a combination of gospel, blues, and jazz played with deep feeling. Born in 1932 in Georgia, Charles became totally blind at age seven. His family moved to Florida where he attended the St. Augustine School for the Blind. Learning to read Braille, memorize music, and to play the piano and clarinet, he played with various musical groups throughout the South and Northwest. Charles created his own style of music in 1954 with his first hit, "My Jesus Is All the World to Me." One of his popular tunes, "I Can't Stop Loving You," sold more than two and a half million records in 1962. Charles was voted one of America's most popular male vocalists of the 1960s in a *Downbeat* magazine poll.

Coleman, Ornette. A black jazz musician of the 1950s and 60s whose trademark was a white plastic saxophone, Ornette Coleman sought a new freedom in music through arrangements which seemed to have little musical order. His style of jazz was compared by critics who enjoyed it to an imitation of the human voice and to meaningless squeaks by many who did not consider it as music. Born in 1930 in Texas, Coleman taught himself to play the alto saxophone by reading instruction books and experimenting by taking his saxophone apart. Before he became popular, Coleman worked at odd jobs for 13 years and used a plastic saxophone since a brass instrument was too expensive. In 1959 he studied at the School of Jazz in Lenox, Massachusetts. Forming a quartet, he and his group made their New York concert debut at Town Hall. Coleman's recordings helped increase his wide popularity.

Aaron Copland

Bing Crosby

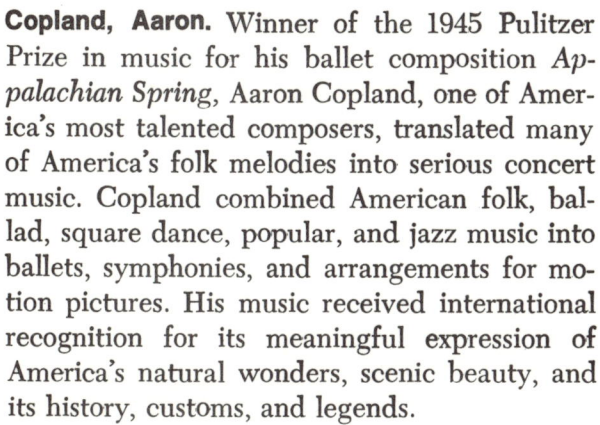

Copland, Aaron. Winner of the 1945 Pulitzer Prize in music for his ballet composition *Appalachian Spring*, Aaron Copland, one of America's most talented composers, translated many of America's folk melodies into serious concert music. Copland combined American folk, ballad, square dance, popular, and jazz music into ballets, symphonies, and arrangements for motion pictures. His music received international recognition for its meaningful expression of America's natural wonders, scenic beauty, and its history, customs, and legends.

Born in Brooklyn in 1900, Copland in his youth studied piano with a sister and by age 15 had decided that he wanted to become a composer. After much study he wrote *The Cat and Mouse* in 1919 and *Symphony for Organ and Orchestra* in 1924. Determined to record America's history in music, Copland used native rhythms in *Music for Theater*, composed in 1925. The same year he became the first composer awarded a Guggenheim Fellowship. He composed *Billy the Kid* (1938) and *Rodeo* (1942) and used folk songs as a basis for the melody in *Lincoln Portrait* (1942). As his reputation grew, Copland became recognized as an authority on American folk history. He composed the musical scores for several motion pictures and in 1949 was voted the Academy Award for his dramatic film score in *The Heiress*. He wrote several books about music in America, including *Our New Music* (1941) and *Copland on Music* (1960). Copland received the Gold Medal for Music in 1956 and the Presidential Medal of Freedom in 1964.

Crosby, Bing (Harry L.) Beginning in the 1930s as a "crooner" of romantic songs, Bing Crosby for more than 40 years won acclaim as one of America's most popular singers and actors on radio, films, records, and television. Born in Washington in 1904, Crosby began his career as a drummer and singer in college bands. After singing in the Rhythm Boys Quartet with the Paul Whiteman Orchestra, his reputation grew and in 1932 Crosby won national popularity as a radio crooner. His bestselling recordings included "Silent Night," "Pennies from Heaven," and "Sweet Leilani." Crosby's recording of "White Christmas" was heard more often than any other record and had sold more than 54 million records by 1970. From the 1930s through the 60s, Crosby appeared in more than 40 musical and comedy films. He won an Academy Award in 1944 for his portrayal of a young priest in *Going My Way*.

DAVIS, Miles—DAVIS, Sammy, Jr.

Miles Davis

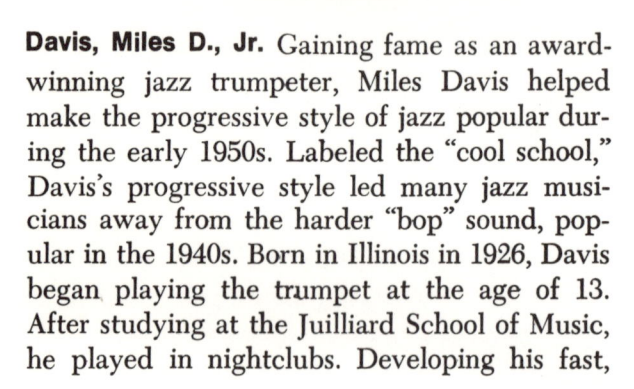

Sammy Davis, Jr.

Davis, Miles D., Jr. Gaining fame as an award-winning jazz trumpeter, Miles Davis helped make the progressive style of jazz popular during the early 1950s. Labeled the "cool school," Davis's progressive style led many jazz musicians away from the harder "bop" sound, popular in the 1940s. Born in Illinois in 1926, Davis began playing the trumpet at the age of 13. After studying at the Juilliard School of Music, he played in nightclubs. Developing his fast, soft style, Davis joined other bands in 1946 and toured the U.S. He formed his own orchestra in the late 1940s and recorded several albums. At the 1955 Newport Jazz Festival, Davis won recognition as one of America's most talented jazz musicians. Readers and critics of *Downbeat* magazine selected him as leading jazz trumpeter of 1959. Through the 1960s and 70s, Davis continued to popularize his cool jazz style in concerts and recordings.

Davis, Sammy, Jr. A versatile dancer, singer and impersonator, Sammy Davis, Jr. entertained American audiences in all mediums of the 20th century, ranging from vaudeville to television. He performed on the stage, in movies and nightclubs, and in addition wrote a bestselling autobiography, *Yes, I Can* in 1965. His films included *Sweet Charity, Oceans 11*, and *Porgy and Bess*. In 1956 he played the leading role in his first Broadway musical, *Mr. Wonderful*, and later he was featured in another Broadway musical, *Golden Boy*.

Born in New York's Harlem in 1925, the black entertainer entered show business when he was four years old as a member of a vaudeville troupe named the Will Mastin Trio. He received little formal education, but he quickly developed a talent for impersonation. When he was six he acted in the movies *Rufus Jones for President* and *Season's Greetings*. In 1943 he began two years of service in the army, spending most of his time writing and directing skits for the soldiers. After his discharge from the army, he returned to the Will Mastin Trio and became its main attraction. In 1954 he issued a song collection *Just For Lovers*, which became one of his most popular albums. As the result of an automobile accident, Davis lost an eye. Despite the injury, he returned to the nightclubs the following year. He produced his own television variety series, made frequent appearances on talk shows, and gave many benefit performances for charity. Among the songs he made popular are "Too Close for Comfort" and "Mr. Wonderful."

William L. Dawson   Dean Dixon   Mattiwilda Dobbs

Dawson, William L. Winning international praise for his choir direction and arrangements of Negro spirituals, black composer and conductor William Dawson contributed many hymns to America's religious music in the mid-1900s. He wrote "My Lord What a Mourning," "I Couldn't Hear Nobody Pray," and an acclaimed symphony, *Negro Folk Symphony No. 1*. Born in Alabama in 1898, Dawson attended Tuskegee Institute until 1921. After studying at Chicago Musical College and the American Conservatory, he worked as a teacher and conductor of several black church choirs. During the 1930s, Dawson was the only black member of the Chicago Civic Orchestra. He rose to international fame in 1934 when conductor Leopold Stokowski presented the world premiere of his *Folk Symphony* in New York's Carnegie Hall. For many years until 1955, Dawson directed the Tuskegee Institute choir.

Dixon, (Charles) Dean. The first black guest conductor of the New York Philharmonic Orchestra, Dean Dixon, beginning in the 1940s, became one of Europe's most celebrated maestros. He was invited to direct many of the world's leading symphony orchestras, including the national orchestras of Austria, Italy, and Israel. Born in New York in 1915, Dean Dixon studied at Juilliard Institute of Musical Art. While a graduate student, he made his first professional appearance, conducting the Music Lovers Chamber Orchestra at New York's Town Hall. In 1948 he won the Alice M. Ditson Award for distinguished service to American music. Unable to obtain permanent appointment as a conductor in the U.S., Dixon moved to Europe in 1949. He served as resident conductor of the Goteborg, Sweden symphony for ten years and in 1962 led the Hessian Radio Symphony of Frankfurt, Germany.

Dobbs, Mattiwilda. Winning international fame as an opera singer, soprano Mattiwilda Dobbs in the early 1950s became the first black singer to perform at La Scala Opera House in Italy. She also performed in featured roles in operas throughout the world, including command performances before the queen of England and the king of Sweden. Born in Georgia in 1925, Miss Dobbs graduated from Spellman College in 1946 and later earned a master's degree in Spanish from Columbia University. She took private voice lessons during her college career and from 1950 to 1952 studied voice in Paris after winning a John Hay Whitney Fellowship. She rose to popularity as the 1950 winner of the International Music Competition in Geneva, Switzerland. After performing her American debut at New York's Town Hall in 1954, Miss Dobbs gave her first American opera performance a year later in San Francisco.

DUNCAN—DYLAN—FELICIANO

Todd Duncan   **Bob Dylan**   **Jose Feliciano**

Duncan, Todd. Winning national popularity as the black actor-singer who first sang Porgy in George Gershwin's folk opera *Porgy and Bess*, Todd Duncan during the 1930s and 40s was among the growing group of black performers who attempted to break down antiblack prejudices in the performing arts. Born in 1903 in Kentucky, Duncan studied music at Butler University, graduated from Columbia with a master's degree in 1925, and began a teaching career. In 1930 he joined Howard University as a professor of voice and became chairman of the music department. His success in *Porgy and Bess* in 1935 led to White House appearances, concert tours, and starring roles in opera and Broadway musicals, including *Cabin in the Sky*. His performance in *Lost in the Stars* won him the Critics Award in 1950 for the best male performance in a Broadway musical. Duncan also appeared in the film *Syncopation*.

Dylan, Bob. Known in the 1960s as "an angry young man with a guitar," folk singer and composer Bob Dylan influenced popular music with his songs protesting war, intolerance, and poverty. Born Robert Zimmerman in Minnesota in 1941, Dylan taught himself to play several musical instruments. Using a country-style dialect, he wrote both lyrics and music for more than 200 songs and performed in night clubs, concert halls, and on college campuses. Playing harmonica accompaniment for a song being recorded in 1961, Dylan was recognized by a musical talent scout for his unusual sound and was hired to record additional songs. In 1965 Dylan combined the folk song style with an electronic beat to create the folk rock sound. His "Blowin in the Wind" and "Mr. Tambourine Man" are among his most popular works. Dylan's unusual musical style continued to be imitated by other popular singers.

Feliciano, Jose. Born sightless, Jose Feliciano taught himself to play the guitar at the age of nine and in 1969 won two Grammy awards for his singing and guitar artistry. He worked out his guitar arrangements with a tape recorder and learned lyrics by Braille. Born in 1945 in Puerto Rico, Feliciano moved to New York City where he attended high school. Starting his career by playing without pay in Greenwich Village coffeehouses, he later received engagements in many small nightclubs throughout the United States and Canada. In 1965 Feliciano released his first solo album, *The Voice and Guitar of Jose Feliciano*, a critical and popular success. Many more albums in his special blues and rock style followed, and in 1969 the album *Souled* reached sales of $1 million within weeks of its release. In addition to records and concerts, Feliciano performed on his own television program.

FIEDLER—FITZGERALD

Arthur Fiedler

Ella Fitzgerald

Fiedler, Arthur. Founder in 1929 of free outdoor symphony concerts that attracted thousands, conductor and musician Arthur Fiedler made serious music popular with millions of listeners who had never attended a formal concert. Born in 1894 in Boston of a musical family, Fiedler studied violin in Europe and at 19 was selected to play with the Boston Symphony Orchestra. Serving briefly in World War I, he returned to organize the Boston Sinfonietta, a group of 25 musicians devoted to chamber music who toured the country and made recordings. His interest in producing free outdoor concerts was realized in 1920, when the first program was performed with Fiedler conducting. The outdoor concerts were soon imitated in most large cities. Fiedler appeared as guest conductor with many orchestras in the U.S. and abroad and was featured on many radio and television programs.

Fitzgerald, Ella. A composer and leading jazz interpreter of popular music, Ella Fitzgerald recorded "A-Tisket A-Tasket" in 1938 and overnight rose to national popularity. Using her voice like an instrument, with effortless changes in musical style, Miss Fitzgerald became known as the First Lady of Song. Born in Virginia in 1918, she was raised in a New York orphanage. Entering a talent contest in Harlem in 1934, she attracted the attention of band leader Chick Webb, who became her coach and helped develop her unique singing style. She remained with his band as a vocalist and became its leader after Webb's death.

Working as a solo singer, Miss Fitzgerald developed into a major attraction in leading theaters and clubs. Touring with Norman Granz and his musical group, her reputation became worldwide as she appeared in Canada, Japan, and Europe. After entertaining at a dinner club in San Francisco in 1955, Miss Fitzgerald appeared in the film, *Pete Kelly's Blues*, and sang the title song. After her performance at the 1956 Newport Jazz Festival, a music critic noted: "She quickly captured the crowd's fancy. They had what they came for and refused to let her go." With sales totalling into the millions, her recordings of "How High the Moon," "That's My Desire," and others are examples of her breathless and free style. Widely known for her albums *Cole Porter Song Book*, *Lullabies of Birdland*, and *Ella Sings Gershwin*, Miss Fitzgerald many times led the *Downbeat* and *Metronome* magazine polls as the leading American female vocalist.

FLORES—FRANKLIN

Pedro Flores

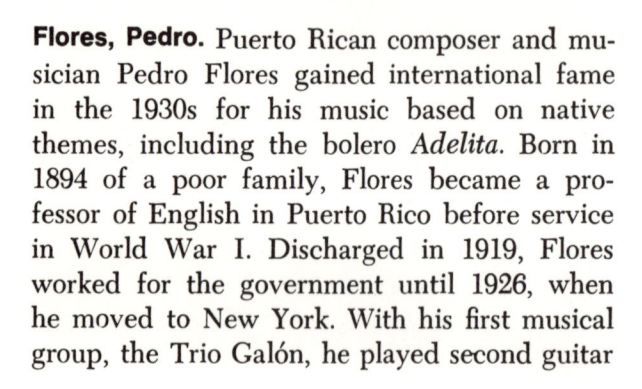

Aretha Franklin

Flores, Pedro. Puerto Rican composer and musician Pedro Flores gained international fame in the 1930s for his music based on native themes, including the bolero *Adelita*. Born in 1894 of a poor family, Flores became a professor of English in Puerto Rico before service in World War I. Discharged in 1919, Flores worked for the government until 1926, when he moved to New York. With his first musical group, the Trio Galón, he played second guitar featuring his lively style and Latin rhythms at many fiestas. Later organizing the Cuarteto Flores, he became the most popular interpreter of Puerto Rican music. Flores made his musical debut in Puerto Rico in 1941. After World War II, Flores disbanded the group and toured Central America to great acclaim. His originality in blending Puerto Rico's native music into modern style brought Flores recognition from many American music critics.

Franklin, Aretha. Combining her own unique talent for rhythm and blues with the spirited, foot-stomping singing style she learned as a gospel singer in her father's church, Aretha Franklin in the 1960s became well known as a black "soul" singer. Many music critics believed her choice of songs and the way she sang them expressed a deeply felt sense of black identity. One of them, "Respect," is sometimes referred to as "the new black national anthem." But Miss Franklin said her music was not for blacks alone but for everyone: "It's not cool to be Negro or Jewish or Italian or anything else. It's just cool to be alive, to be around. You don't have to be Negro to have soul." Miss Franklin in 1967 received a standing ovation in an appearance at New York's Philharmonic Hall, and in 1971 and 1972 won the Grammy Award as the best rhythm and blues singer.

Born in Memphis, Tennessee in 1942, Miss Franklin became a soloist in her father's church choir at age twelve. She made her first recording of gospel songs at fourteen. Moving to New York in 1961 to seek a career as a vocalist, she began to achieve popularity during the late 1960s after signing a contract with a recording company that specialized in rhythm and blues singers. Arranging her own music and composing many original songs, Miss Franklin performed all over Europe and throughout the United States. Many of her albums, including *I Never Loved a Man* (1967), *Lady Soul* (1968), and *Aretha Now* (1968), sold more than a million records.

GARNER—GILLESPIE—GOODMAN

Erroll Garner **Dizzy Gillespie** **Benny Goodman**

Garner, Erroll. Judged the world's number one jazz pianist by a poll of international music critics in 1957, Erroll Garner created unique jazz sounds that stressed strong melody, deep bass rhythms, and brilliant improvisations. His most popular compositions include the songs "Misty" and "Laura." Born in Pittsburgh in 1921, Garner began playing piano at the age of six. He never learned to read music, but became adept at playing by ear. Later Garner joined a dance orchestra and performed in New York City nightclubs. His album *Down By the Sea* sold more than a million copies. He was the first jazz musician to give a solo recital at Cleveland's Music Hall and to perform a special concert of his compositions with the Cleveland Symphony Orchestra. Describing his technique of improvisation, Garner wrote, "I just hear a sound coming into my head, and hope to catch it with my hands."

Gillespie, Dizzy (John Birks). The first jazz band leader to officially represent America abroad, black trumpeter Dizzy Gillespie in 1956 took his orchestra on a tour across Europe and Asia sponsored by the U.S. State Department. In the early 1940s, Gillespie developed and helped popularize bebop, a variation of jazz that used fast, complicated flights of notes to enliven the melody. Born in 1917 in Cheraw, South Carolina, Gillespie later received the nickname Dizzy for his undisciplined actions on stage. Organizing a band at age 14, he won a scholarship to study music. After playing with leading bands, he formed his own group in 1945 and developed the unique style that brought him international acclaim. Reorganizing his band in 1946, Gillespie was honored the following year with an invitation to perform in Carnegie Hall, Gillespie in 1956 won the *Downbeat* award as the outstanding trumpeter.

Goodman, Benny (Benjamin D.). When dancers in Los Angeles in 1935 crowded around the bandstand to listen to the new and exciting jazz style of clarinetist Benny Goodman, the era of swing music began in the U.S. Wherever he played, Goodman drew large audiences, and soon he was known as the King of Swing. Born 1909 in Chicago, Goodman learned to play the clarinet at a synagogue and later at Hull House, a neighborhood settlement. He played clarinet with many popular dance bands and in 1934 formed his own group and toured the country. His unique music style was not quickly accepted until he reached California, where he was received as the innovator of the new jazz sound. In 1938 he conducted a jazz concert in Carnegie Hall and later performed as a classical clarinetist with string quartets and symphonies. Goodman also toured the Far East and the Soviet Union.

HAMPTON—HARRIS—HAYES

Lionel Hampton **Roy Harris** **Roland Hayes**

Hampton, Lionel. Popularizing the "electric" sound in music, black musician Lionel Hampton in the 1930s created a new interest in jazz by introducing the vibraharp, or vibes—an electrical instrument built and played like the xylophone. The vibes produced pulsating and bell-like sounds. For more than 40 years, Hampton pioneered the use of the vibes as a solo instrument in songs such as "Flying Home." Born in Alabama in 1914, Hampton first learned to play the drums in high school. After studying music at the University of Southern California, Hampton during the 1930s played the drums with Les Hite's group, where he learned to play the vibes. After four years with the Benny Goodman Quartet, he formed his own group in 1940 and soon became one of the leading jazz musicians of the big band era. In the 1960s, Hampton formed a smaller group called the Inner Circle and made a worldwide tour.

Harris, Roy. Combining traditional American folk ballads with legends from U.S. history, Roy Harris, beginning in the 1920s, composed concert music to portray the drama and adventure of America. Born in an Oklahoma log cabin in 1898, Harris began writing music at age 24. After studying in Paris for three years, he returned to the U.S. in 1929. Harris won national acclaim when his *First Symphony* (1933) was performed by the Boston Symphony Orchestra. Soon afterward, he composed the overture *When Johnny Comes Marching Home* (1934), the symphony *Farewell to Pioneers* (1935), and two of his most popular symphonies, *Third Symphony* (1938) and *The Folk Song Symphony* (1939). Harris served on the faculties of several universities and helped organize the first Pittsburgh International Contemporary Music Festival in 1952. His colorful and dramatic style inspired many later composers.

Hayes, Roland. Considered by some authorities to be one of the great America-born tenors, black singer Roland Hayes helped break down the barriers that prevented blacks from performing on America's concert stages in the early 1900s. Born in Georgia in 1887, Hayes sang in church choirs until he heard tenor Enrico Caruso's records, which inspired him to study voice. Entering Fisk University in 1905, he received music training and later joined the Fisk Jubilee Singers. Hayes sponsored two of his own recitals in Boston Symphony Hall in 1917 and in 1920 moved to Europe for further study. In 1921 the king and queen of England requested a command performance. Hayes returned to America to find many concert halls opened to him. Winner of the Spingarn Medal (1924) and the French Purple Ribbon in 1949, Hayes was appointed to Boston University's school of music faculty in 1950.

Jascha Heifetz • Florence Henderson • Earl Hines

Heifetz, Jascha. Recognized for his outstanding technique and flawless performances, concert violinist Jascha Heifetz began appearing as a soloist in Russia at the age of seven and gave his first American concert in 1917. Born in Russia in 1901, Heifetz learned to play the violin from his father. At the age of four he was accepted at the Royal School of Music in Russia. Showing unusual talent, he studied at the St. Petersburg Conservatory under the famous teacher Leopold Auer and soon played throughout Russia. In 1914 Heifetz became a soloist with the Berlin Philharmonic. After immigrating to America, he performed in cities throughout the world and often entertained Allied soldiers during World War II. Believing that motion pictures were an educational medium, Heifetz in 1939 appeared in *They Shall Have Music*. He continued to appear in concerts all over the world through the early 1970s.

Henderson, Florence. Starring in musical comedies on Broadway, in motion pictures, and on television, Florence Henderson, beginning in the 1950s, became one of America's popular entertainers. In 1961-62 she was featured in a traveling production of *The Sound of Music* and in 1969 was chosen to costar in the television comedy, "The Brady Bunch." Born in Indiana in 1934, Miss Henderson moved to New York City in 1951 to begin a singing career. In 1952 she won her first major role, playing Laurey in a road production of *Oklahoma!* The following year, she won the leading part in the musical comedy *Fanny*. Warmly praised by drama and music critics, Miss Henderson was featured in several more musicals, including *South Pacific* (1964), and appeared on many national television programs. Chosen for a leading role in her first motion picture, Miss Henderson played Nina in the 1970 film, *Song of Norway*.

Hines, Earl. Recognized as one of America's most talented jazz pianists during the 1930s and 40s, Earl "Fatha" Hines popularized the "trumpet style" of piano playing. He created a sharp trumpet sound by playing irregular high notes with his right hand and rhythmic bass chords with his left. Born in Pennsylvania in 1905, Hines learned to play the trumpet from his father, but turned to the piano because trumpet notes hurt his ears. He began his professional music career in the early 1920s, playing in Pittsburgh nightclubs. Hines soon moved to Chicago, where he made several recordings with Louis Armstrong. In 1928 Hines formed his own band and toured the U.S. He composed many of his most popular songs, including "Rosetta," "Harlem Laments," and "The Earl." During the 1950s, Hines played with Armstrong and performed in foreign countries. His style achieved popularity again in the 1960s and 70s.

HORNE—HOROWITZ

Lena Horne

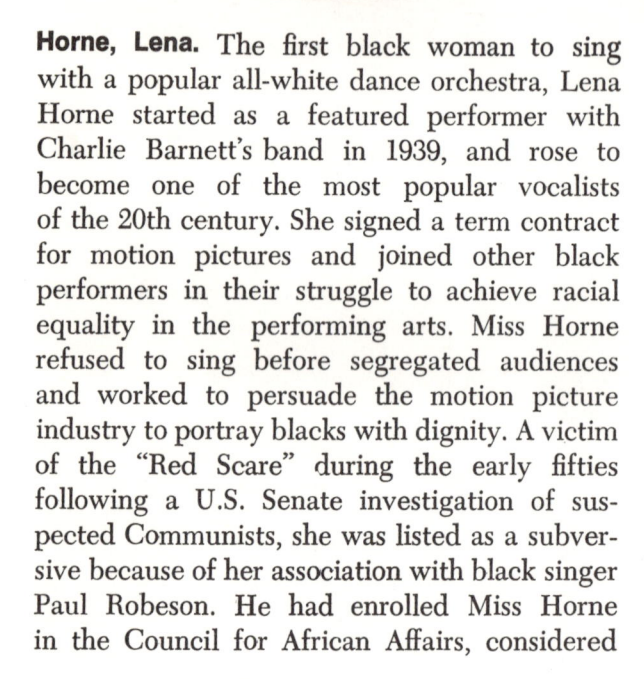

Vladimir Horowitz

Horne, Lena. The first black woman to sing with a popular all-white dance orchestra, Lena Horne started as a featured performer with Charlie Barnett's band in 1939, and rose to become one of the most popular vocalists of the 20th century. She signed a term contract for motion pictures and joined other black performers in their struggle to achieve racial equality in the performing arts. Miss Horne refused to sing before segregated audiences and worked to persuade the motion picture industry to portray blacks with dignity. A victim of the "Red Scare" during the early fifties following a U.S. Senate investigation of suspected Communists, she was listed as a subversive because of her association with black singer Paul Robeson. He had enrolled Miss Horne in the Council for African Affairs, considered a Communist-front organization. Although found innocent of subversion, Miss Horne for several years was unable to obtain work.

Born in Brooklyn in 1917, Miss Horne accompanied her actress mother on theatrical tours throughout the South. Joining the chorus line at Harlem's Cotton Club in 1941 when she was 16, she achieved her first success as a night club performer with her rendition of such classics as "The Man I Love" and "Embraceable You." Her outstanding films include *Cabin in the Sky* (1943) and *Stormy Weather* (1943). When the Communist scare ended, she returned to her singing career as the featured attraction in her first musical, *Jamaica*, a 1957 hit. In 1970 Lena Horne won critical acclaim for her many appearances on television.

Horowitz, Vladimir. A pianist who gained international popularity in the 20th century for his acknowledged mastery, Vladimir Horowitz delighted audiences throughout the world with his intensity and skill in playing difficult compositions. Born in Russia in 1904, Horowitz began playing the piano at the age of four. Although studying for a career as a composer, financial difficulties caused Horowitz in 1922 to play piano professionally. Traveling to New York, he first performed for American audiences in 1928, displaying his unique ability in many styles of piano solos. Forced to retire temporarily in 1953 because of poor health, Horowitz returned to the concert stage in 1965. Beginning in 1931, his musical performances were recorded, and his records were so popular that Horowitz became the first recording artist to win a Grammy award in each of four consecutive years from 1962 to 1965.

Burl Ives   **B. B. King**   **John Lewis**

Ives, Burl. Internationally known as a folk singer of classic American ballads, Burl Ives also won recognition starting in the 1940s as a distinguished stage and screen actor. Born in Illinois in 1909, Ives traveled throughout the U.S. in the 1930s collecting folk songs of lumberjacks, cowboys, fishermen and steelworkers. He sang in concerts in Europe and America and compiled his popular music in several collections, including *Tales of America* (1954). Appearing in Broadway musicals in the late 1930s and 40s, he received the Donaldson Award as the best supporting actor for his role in *Sing Out Sweet Land* (1944). After moving to Hollywood in 1945 to appear in the movie *Smoky*, he won an Academy of Motion Picture Arts and Sciences award in 1958 for his dramatic role in *The Big Country* and was praised for his performance in *Cat on a Hot Tin Roof* (1958).

King, B. B. (Riley). A self-taught master of the electric guitar, B.B. King during the 1960s became one of the first black musicians to popularize with white audiences the style of music known as the blues. Musicians described the blues as melodies of African origin and based on the singing of black field hands. King's style of playing the blues, using the guitar almost as an added voice rather than accompaniment, was later imitated by many rock guitar players. Born Riley King in Mississippi in 1925, he began playing the guitar in his early teens and by 1927 was a disk jockey, singer, and guitarist in Memphis, Tennessee. Known as Blues Boy, King shortened the name to B.B. Often unpaid, for nearly 20 years he played his unique style of blues on one-night stands in small black night clubs. But when British rock groups began to feature the blues in recordings, King soon became a favorite of white audiences.

Lewis, John. A pioneer in the development of jazz music, John Lewis won international acclaim during the mid-1900s as an arranger, conductor, composer, and pianist. In 1952 Lewis cofounded the Modern Jazz Quartet, a group that was to receive worldwide praise and perform at classical music festivals where jazz groups had seldom been invited. Born in 1920 in Illinois, Lewis in 1945 joined a leading jazz band as arranger and pianist. His first major work was *Toccata for Trumpet and Orchestra*, introduced by Dizzy Gillespie at a 1947 Carnegie Hall concert. Among the hundreds of songs composed by Lewis are his popular "Django" and "European Windows." His many albums include *Third Stream Jazz* and *John Lewis, The Wonderful World of Jazz*. In 1958 and 1959 Lewis served as music director of the Monterey Jazz Festival in California, and he also taught music.

LOPEZ—McKUEN—MATHIS

Trini Lopez   **Rod McKuen**   **Johnny Mathis**

Lopez, Trini. One of America's leading recording artists of the 1960s and early 70s, Trini Lopez introduced a new and unique style of singing called Latin folk-rock. His style combined smooth, lively singing with rock n' roll and Spanish-accented rhythms. His most popular recording, "If I Had A Hammer," sold over four million records in 1963. Born in Texas in 1937, Lopez taught himself to play the guitar at the age of 11. During his teens he formed a combo that played in Dallas nightclubs. Moving to Los Angeles in 1960, Lopez turned soloist, and as his popularity grew, he started recording. His first album *Trini Lopez at P.J.'s* (1963) was an immediate success, selling more than a million records. After a European tour in 1964, Lopez returned to the U.S. and soon appeared in leading nightclubs. Lopez also costarred in the motion picture *The Dirty Dozen* (1963). His other albums include *The Latin Album*.

McKuen, Rod. Composing many songs and poems that dramatize the feelings of loneliness and alienation of American youth in the mid-20th century, Rod McKuen achieved wide popularity singing and reciting his works. While many reviewers criticized the quality of his writing, most agreed that his sincere performing style held great emotional appeal for his audiences. Born in California in 1933, McKuen left school at age 11 and worked at odd jobs on the West Coast until he became a disc jockey in his late teens. He began to discuss his own problems on the air in his late-night show "Rendezvous with Rod." His listeners responded by seeking advice on their problems, and the show established McKuen's image as a warm, sympathetic performer. His best-selling books include *The World of Rod McKuen* and *In Someone's Shadows*. Among his most popular songs are "Jean" and "If You Go Away."

Mathis, Johnny. Singing romantic ballads in the late 1950s while other performers were following the trend to rock and roll rhythm, black vocalist Johnny Mathis perfected a warm, mellow musical style that made him widely popular for many years. Born in San Francisco in 1935, Mathis was a student and outstanding athlete at San Francisco State College in 1955. When the owner of a local nightclub heard him sing in an informal jam session, he induced Mathis to become an entertainer. After his appearance in several clubs, Mathis signed a contract with a prominent recording firm, and his recordings sold millions of records. In the 1960s and 70s he appeared in movies and on television and gave concerts in America and Europe. Interested in helping other blacks, Mathis donated part of his earnings to the National Association for the Advancement of Colored People and the Southern Christian Leadership Conference.

Shigemi Matsumoto **Dorothy Maynor** **Gian-Carlo Menotti**

Matsumoto, Shigemi. Achieving recognition in the operatic world at the age of 22, soprano Shigemi Matsumoto won first prize in the 1968 San Francisco Opera auditions and became the only Japanese member of the opera company. Born in 1946 in Colorado, Miss Matsumoto won the Metropolitan Opera's regional audition in 1967 and for two years was selected as guest artist with Arthur Fiedler's "Pops" concerts. After graduation in 1968 from California State University, Miss Matsumoto performed with many opera groups, including Spring Opera Theater, Western Opera Theater, and Portland Opera Company. Her roles included Rosina in *The Barber of Seville,* Barbarina in *The Marriage of Figaro,* both Mimi and Musette in *La Boheme,* and Norina in *Don Pasquale.* She was selected soloist for the concert celebrating the 25th anniversary of the founding of the United Nations.

Maynor, Dorothy. Appearing as a concert soloist with almost every major symphony orchestra in America, black soprano Dorothy Maynor won the highest praise of music critics for her first concert in New York's Town Hall in 1939. Born in Virginia in 1910, Miss Maynor was the daughter of a Methodist minister and started singing in her father's church choir. Entering the Hampton Institute to study teaching, she toured Europe and America with the Hampton Institute Choir, and later attended Westminster Choir College. After meeting Serge Koussevitzky, conductor of the Boston Symphony Orchestra, at the Berkshire Music Festival in 1939, she persuaded him to listen to her voice. Calling her singing a "musical revelation," Koussevitzky said "the whole world must hear her" and engaged her to sing with the Boston Symphony. Miss Maynor toured America and Europe, and appeared on radio and television.

Menotti, Gian-Carlo. Considered one of the most outstanding composers of the 20th century, Gian-Carlo Menotti won two Pulitzer Prizes for music for his contemporary dramatic operas *The Consul* in 1950 and for *The Saint of Bleecker Street* in 1955. Menotti's popular Christmas opera, *Amahl and the Night Visitors* (1951) was performed annually on television for more than two decades. Born in Italy in 1911, Menotti began to compose music at age six. Moving to the United States in 1928, he enrolled at the Curtis Institute of Music in Philadelphia, where he composed his opera, *Amelia Goes to the Ball,* which was performed in the U.S. in 1937. In 1946 Menotti presented his operas *The Telephone* and *The Medium* on Broadway and won high critical praise for combining beautiful music with exciting drama. Menotti helped establish an annual summer festival of music in Spoleto, Italy.

MONTOYA—MOORE—ORMANDY

Carlos Montoya   **Russell Moore**   **Eugene Ormandy**

Montoya, Carlos. An inventive flamenco guitarist in the mid-20th century, Carlos Montoya became the first to perform flamenco music as a soloist rather than an accompanist to singers and dancers. He introduced the flamenco music of Spain to Americans. He also composed the first flamenco suite for full orchestra, *Suite Flamenco,* in 1966. Montoya was born in Madrid, Spain in 1903, the son of Spanish gypsies. His mother taught him to play the guitar when he was eight years old, and he learned the difficult flamenco music by watching outstanding guitarists in cafes. By the age of fourteen he had become a skilled accompanist himself. From 1928 until 1945 he toured Europe, the Far East, and the United States, accompanying outstanding flamenco dancers, including the well-known La Argentinita. Montoya later became a soloist, playing flamenco guitar on the concert stage.

Moore, Russell. A Pima Indian who first imitated the music of the mission school band by playing on a piece of pipe with holes in it, Russell "Big Chief" Moore rose to become an internationally acclaimed trombonist during the mid-1900s. Born on an Arizona reservation in 1912, Moore was sent to Chicago at the age of 11 to live with an uncle, a music teacher, who taught him piano and brass instruments. After learning the trombone at a government school, he began his musical career; he achieved recognition after joining Lionel Hampton's band in 1935. Moore toured the country with Louis Armstrong and was featured in Armstrong's hit recording of "Hello Dolly." He later led several bands of his own and toured Europe, Asia, Africa, and Australia. Moore entertained at the White House and played for the inaugural balls of Presidents Kennedy and Johnson.

Ormandy, Eugene. As permanent conductor of the Philadelphia Symphony Orchestra in the mid-20th century, Eugene Ormandy developed it into one of the finest and best-known orchestras in the world. He made many recordings with the orchestra and led the group on several foreign tours. Born in Budapest, Hungary in 1899, Ormandy began to study the violin when he was five. He toured central Europe as a concert violinist in his teens before traveling to America in 1921 to act as concert master of the Capitol Theatre orchestra in New York City. Ormandy served as guest conductor of the New York Philharmonic and in 1931-1936 was permanent conductor of the Minneapolis Symphony Orchestra. He succeeded Leopold Stokowski as permanent conductor of the Philadelphia Symphony Orchestra. Ormandy was known for his interpretation of 19th-century music.

PEERCE—PETERS—PRESLEY

Jan Peerce   **Roberta Peters**   **Elvis Presley**

Peerce, Jan. An international operatic performer, tenor Jan Peerce sang throughout the world during the mid-1900s. Born in New York in 1904, Peerce earned his college tuition money by playing the violin in orchestras. He made his New York debut in 1939 as a tenor with the National Broadcasting Company Symphony, directed by Arturo Toscanini. Two years later, Peerce made his Metropolitan Opera debut. Able to sing popular as well as operatic and light classical music, he made many appearances on Radio City Music Hall broadcasts and was a frequent guest on other radio and television programs. He played leading roles in operas for both the Metropolitan and San Francisco opera companies. He made a tour of Russia under auspices of the State Department and performed in Australia, Africa, and Europe. Peerce was elected the favorite male singer in the U.S. in 1946.

Peters, Roberta. Asked to substitute in a leading role in the opera *Don Giovanni* five hours before its performance in 1950, coloratura soprano Roberta Peters gave an outstanding rendition of Zerlina that started her career as one of the leading voices at the Metropolitan Opera. Although she had never sung on a professional stage or rehearsed with the orchestra, Miss Peters's performance was rewarded with standing ovations and favorable reviews. During her 23-year career with the Metropolitan, she mastered 20 heroines' roles and became known as the Metropolitan's "most celebrated pinchhitter." Born in New York in 1930, Miss Peters studied with opera teacher and coach William Hermann. After being accepted to sing at the Metropolitan, Miss Peters was enrolled in a special training school. Among her most popularly acclaimed roles was the Queen of the Night in *Die Zauberflöte*.

Presley, Elvis A. One of the first country and western singers to combine his music with rhythm and blues, Elvis Presley helped establish and popularize the rock 'n' roll style that became the music of America's youth in the 1950s. The primitive beat of rock 'n' roll, combined with Presley's husky singing voice, lively guitar playing, and body movements, found eager acceptance among teenagers. His personal appearances were met with unprecedented teenage approval. Born in Mississippi in 1935, Presley sang in church choirs as a child and taught himself to play the guitar. His first recording was heard by the president of a recording company, who signed Presley to a contract. He made twenty-one records that each sold more than one million copies. Presley's best-selling songs include "Heartbreak Hotel" and "Blue Suede Shoes." He remained as one of the leading entertainers in the 1970s.

PRICE—ROBESON

Leontyne Price

Price, Leontyne. Making her New York debut at the Metropolitan Opera in 1961, singing the role of Countess Leonora in *Il Trovatore*, lyric soprano Leontyne Price was acclaimed for her remarkable tone and range by critics and the public. Miss Price received one of the largest ovations in Metropolitan Opera history and earned an invitation to open the 1961-1962 opera season. Born Mary Leontine Price in 1927 in Mississippi, she attended local schools and in 1944 enrolled at Central State College in Ohio, intending to become a school music teacher. Her vocal talent was quickly recognized during her college years, and she was encouraged to seek a singing career. After graduation in 1948, Miss Price won a scholarship to New York's Juilliard School of Music.

Miss Price's performance in a Juilliard production of *Falstaff* was witnessed by composer Virgil Thompson, who selected her in 1952 for his Broadway musical *Four Saints in Three Acts*. Her singing and acting talent won her the role of Bess in the 1952 revival of George Gershwin's *Porgy and Bess*, in which she appeared for two years. In 1957 Miss Price made her operatic debut in *Dialogues of the Carmelites* with the San Francisco Opera Company. She later made return appearances in the title role of *Aida*, as Leonora in *Il Trovatore*, and as Donna Elvira in *Don Giovanni*. In 1960 she appeared at the La Scala opera in Italy and sang the leading role in *Aida* without rehearsals. In 1965 she won the NAACP Spingarn Award. Miss Price continued to sing leading roles into the 1970s.

Paul Robeson

Robeson, Paul. An All-American football player and outstanding student, Paul Robeson began his career in 1923 as a lawyer, but changed to the stage and gained world popularity as an actor and singer. He earned more than $100,000 a year in the 1940s in Hollywood and on Broadway and as a concert performer and recording artist. He spoke out forcefully against racial prejudice long before civil rights activism became widespread. His attacks damaged his popularity, and the U.S. State Department, accusing him of being a Communist, cancelled his passport in 1950. When the Supreme Court ordered his passport restored in 1958, Robeson left for Europe, remaining there until 1963, when illness brought him back to the U.S. to live in retirement.

Robeson was born in New Jersey in 1898. He was awarded a scholarship in 1915 to Rutgers University, where he earned 12 athletic letters and honors for scholarship, oratory, and debating. He worked his way through Columbia Law School by playing professional football, but found law practice boring. He first acted in a Harlem YWCA production, then with the Provincetown Players in Greenwich Village. He became friendly with playwright Eugene O'Neill and played leading roles in O'Neill's *Emperor Jones* and *All God's Chillun Got Wings*. Encouraged by his wife, Robeson started his concert-singing career in 1925. A New York production of *Othello* in 1943 brought him his outstanding triumph and an ovation described as "one of the most prolonged and wildest . . . in the history of the New York theater."

Richard Rodgers

Artur Rubinstein

Rodgers, Richard. A talented composer of Broadway musicals and popular songs for four decades, Richard Rodgers combined drama and music with purely American source material and created a new and unique American art form in the Pulitzer Prize-winning musical plays *Oklahoma* (1944) and *South Pacific* (1949). Rodgers was also credited with developing the plot song, in which the music and lyrics of each song in a play advance the movement of the story. Collaborating with lyricist Lorenz Hart until shortly before Hart's death in 1943, Rodgers then began a 17-year association with Oscar Hammerstein II, producing musical plays, including *Carousel* (1945), *The King and I* (1951), and *The Sound of Music* (1959).

Rodgers was born in New York City in 1902 and as a 16-year old freshman submitted the winning score for Columbia University's annual varsity show. During its production, he met Lorenz Hart, and the two began writing songs for Broadway musicals in 1919, achieving their first success in 1925. Collaborating on more than twenty productions from 1925 to 1942, their songs include "Where or When," "With a Song in My Heart," and "Bewitched, Bothered and Bewildered." When Hart withdrew from the production of *Oklahoma* in 1942, Rodgers began working with Hammerstein. Together they wrote many of America's most memorable and popular songs: "Some Enchanted Evening," "Hello Young Lovers," "Younger than Springtime," and "If I Loved You."

Rubinstein, Artur. Starting as a child prodigy, pianist Artur Rubinstein made his concert debut in 1901 at the age of 12 and later won recognition as one of the outstanding musicians of the 20th century. Born in Poland in 1889, Rubinstein was enrolled in the Warsaw Conservatory at the age of 8. In 1906 he made his American debut at Carnegie Hall. Receiving little acclaim, Rubinstein returned to Europe to further his musical study. In 1910 Rubinstein reappeared on the concert stage in Europe, where he was enthusiastically received. He returned to the U.S. in 1919 but again received little praise from American critics. After performing throughout Europe, Rubinstein retired to restudy the music he had played for nearly 40 years. Adding new discipline to his arrangements, he returned in 1937 for his third and triumphant appearance at Carnegie Hall. Rubinstein became a U.S. citizen in 1946.

SCHUMAN—SEEGER—SERKIN

William Schuman   Pete Seeger   Rudolf Serkin

Schuman, William Howard. The winner in 1943 of the first Pulitzer Prize ever awarded for music, William Schuman helped promote America's creative arts by combining his outstanding organizational abilities with his talent as a composer. Named president of the Lincoln Center for the Performing Arts in 1962, he had earlier served as president of the Juilliard School of Music (1945-61). Schuman was born in New York City in 1910. He decided to study music seriously at age 19, receiving an M.A. in music from Columbia University in 1937, and taught music at Sarah Lawrence College from 1935 until 1945. He always set aside a portion of his time for composing, and in addition to his Pulitzer Prize for *A Free Song* in 1943, he was awarded two Guggenheim Fellowships and a grant from the Metropolitan Opera. After retiring from the Lincoln Center post in 1968, he devoted his full time to composing.

Seeger, Pete. Helping to revive folk music as a popular American musical style, Pete Seeger was active in every form of folk music in the 1940s and 50s—collecting and composing, performing for records, appearing on radio and television and in concerts. Born into a musical family in New York in 1919, Seeger was attracted to folk music after attending a folk festival in 1935. In 1948 Seeger started the widely acclaimed Weavers, in which he sang and played the banjo. The group appeared in night clubs, concert halls, and theaters. Considered an authority on the banjo, he wrote an instruction manual in 1948. In 1955 he refused to testify before a congressional committee investigating communism. Charged with contempt of Congress, he was cleared in 1962. Among the songs he composed by himself or with others are "Where Have All the Flowers Gone?" and "If I Had a Hammer."

Serkin, Rudolf. Acclaimed a musical genius at four years of age, Rudolf Serkin rose to become a leading concert pianist, musical director, and teacher in the mid-1900s. Born in 1903 in Bohemia (later Czechoslovakia), Serkin studied piano and at twelve made his European debut as guest artist with the Vienna Symphony Orchestra. After his successful concert, Serkin was offered a series of concert tours which he refused, insisting on further study and practice. At the age of 17, he performed on his first European concert tour and appeared with violinist-composer Adolf Busch in a series of sonatas for violin and piano. Serkin made his American debut in 1933 at the Coolidge Festival in Washington, D.C., and in 1934 he appeared with the New York Philharmonic Orchestra. Founder and director of the Marlboro, Vermont summer music festival, Serkin was appointed a director of the Curtis Music Institute in 1939.

Beverly Sills

Sills, Beverly. Praised by music critics throughout the world in the 1960s as an outstanding coloratura soprano, Beverly Sills was one of the first internationally acclaimed opera singers to receive all of her music training in the United States. Beginning her career at the age of three on a children's radio program, she studied, performed, and worked for more than twenty years until she became one of the most highly praised performers with the New York City Opera Company. Enduring the personal tragedy of having one retarded and one nearly deaf child, Miss Sills believed that learning to cope with her grief helped develop her abilities as an actress and as a singer.

Born Belle Silverman in New York in 1929, Miss Sills made her first radio appearance in 1932 as Bubbles Silverman. She became a regular performer on the "Major Bowes Family Hour" radio show and the radio serial "Our Gal Sunday." Miss Sills stopped performing when she was twelve and devoted the following four years to her schoolwork, language and music lessons, and to intensive voice lessons under the well-known teacher Estelle Liebling. She began touring the U.S. in 1945 with several performing companies and after nine auditions over a three-year period was finally accepted as a soprano with the New York City Opera in 1953. Her performance as Cleopatra in Handel's *Julius Caesar* and as Manon in Massenet's *Manon* won her high praise from American opera critics, and her performances throughout the 1960s and early 1970s earned her critical acclaim.

Frank Sinatra

Sinatra, Frank. Starting as a band singer in 1939, Frank Sinatra rose to become a leading American recording artist, actor, and music publisher in a career that extended over 35 years by the 1970s. An active supporter of charitable and humanitarian causes, Sinatra made numerous appearances before fund-raising groups, dedications, and correctional institutions. Born in 1917 in New Jersey, Sinatra attended public schools and studied music at Drake Institute. He joined the Tommy Dorsey band in 1939, and his personal singing style made him popular with teen-age girls. He became a solo performer in 1942, appearing in clubs and theaters, and recording many popular songs. He appeared in the motion picture *Anchors Aweigh* in 1945, and for his film role in *From Here to Eternity*, Sinatra won a motion picture Academy Award in 1953. Sinatra briefly retired from singing and acting in 1971.

SMITH—STEWART—STILL

Kate Smith   **Albert Stewart**   **William G. Still**

Smith, Kate. One of America's most popular singers during the 1930s, Kate Smith made her professional debut in 1926 and 47 years later still attracted capacity audiences. Born Kathryn Smith in Virginia in 1909, she made her first professional appearance at 17 in a Broadway musical, *Honeymoon Lane.* Discovered by an artists' representative who became her manager, she soon became the leading radio singer of the 1930s, adopting as her theme song "When the Moon Comes Over the Mountain." In 1938 she persuaded composer Irving Berlin to give her exclusive rights to sing his "God Bless America" song on the air. She helped make the song one of the most popular patriotic songs ever written. During World War II, Miss Smith helped raise more than $600 million in war bonds and several million for the American Red Cross. Miss Smith made more than 2,000 recordings—more than any other singer.

Stewart, Albert. To help preserve the culture of the Chickasaw Indians, Albert Stewart lectured on Indian music and sang before audiences at more than 5,000 schools, colleges, and clubs in the mid-1900s. Born in Oklahoma in 1909, Stewart was a grandnephew of Chickasaw Chief Ton-Tubbe and of Choctaw Chief Moshala Tubbee and related to Frances Folsom, wife of President Grover Cleveland. He worked his way through Chicago Musical College and Roosevelt University by singing and in 1939 was named a winner at the Chicago Music Festival. A student of Indian song and folklore, Stewart popularized Indian music on children's television programs and in the motion picture *Rhythm,* produced for schools. He was also a featured singer at Indian ceremonials in the Wisconsin Dells. An active member in the Indian Council Fire, Stewart twice served as its president.

Still, William Grant. One of America's outstanding classical composers and the first black to conduct a major American orchestra, William Grant Still began his career in 1915 as a jazz musician and arranger. In the 1920s he started to compose symphony music, drawing his themes from jazz, work songs, blues, and spirituals. Born in Mississippi in 1895, Still studied science at Wilberforce University, but he hoped to become a composer. He left school to earn money by playing in dance bands, and a small legacy helped him enroll at Oberlin Conservatory of Music in 1916. After service in the navy in World War I, Still studied composition in New York and Boston, winning acclaim in 1931 for his *Afro-American Symphony*. In 1936 he conducted the Los Angeles Philharmonic orchestra at the Hollywood Bowl in a program of his compositions. Still also wrote operas and film scores.

SUZUKI—TUCKER—VAN HEUSEN

Pat Suzuki **Richard Tucker** **James Van Heusen**

Suzuki, Pat. After achieving wide popularity in 1958 for her record albums and appearances on American and Canadian television, Pat Suzuki gained additional recognition by her stage role in the Rodgers and Hammerstein production *Flower Drum Song*. Born on a California farm in 1931, Miss Suzuki was the daughter of first generation Japanese-American parents. When the U.S. declared war on Japan in 1941, she was placed in an internment camp with her family and other Japanese-Americans living in the western U.S. After the war, Miss Suzuki attended several colleges, paying for her education by singing in supper clubs. She graduated from San Jose State College in 1954 and moved to New York in 1957 to enter the entertainment profession. After her outstanding performance in *Flower Drum Song*, she toured the U.S. in the musical *The Owl and the Pussycat* and ap- in the movie *Skullduggery* in 1969.

Tucker, Richard. Starting his singing career at age 6 in a synagogue choir, Richard Tucker became one of the leading tenors of the world, appearing in opera houses on four continents in the mid-1900s. Born in Brooklyn in 1913, Tucker worked at various jobs after graduating from high school while studying singing under Paul Althouse, a former opera singer and noted teacher. Tucker made his concert debut at New York's Town Hall in 1939 and his opera debut at the Metropolitan in 1945 in the role of Enzo in *La Gioconda*. In 1949 he sang the role of Radames in *Aida*, presented on radio and television by Arturo Toscanini. Tucker was the first American invited to make official recordings at Milan's La Scala opera house, where he sang in 1954 and 1955. Throughout his career he was a synagogue cantor. Tucker continued as a leading opera tenor and sang numerous roles at the Metropolitan during the 1970s. He died in 1975.

Van Heusen, James. One of the outstanding songwriters of the mid-1900s, James Van Heusen composed popular music that won him four motion picture Academy Awards. Born Edward Babcock in 1913 in New York, he was expelled from two schools before becoming a disk jockey at sixteen. To keep his job hidden from his father, he changed his name to Van Heusen. After studying music for two years at Syracuse University, Van Heusen wrote several hit songs in 1938-39, and in one week three of his songs were on the Hit Parade. Impressed by his song "Imagination," Bing Crosby hired him to write music for *The Road to Zanzibar* (1941). For the film *Going My Way*, he wrote, with Johnny Burke, "Swinging on a Star," which won him his first Academy Award (1944). Other award winners, all written with Sammy Cahn, were "All the Way," (1957), "High Hopes" (1959), and "Call Me Irresponsible" (1963).

VAUGHAN—WALLENSTEIN—WARFIELD

Sarah Vaughan   **Alfred Wallenstein**   **William Warfield**

Vaughan, Sarah. A singer whose unique voice range enabled her to present jazz and popular songs in her own personal style, Sarah Vaughan was voted the leading female vocalist of the U.S. for six consecutive years between 1947 and 1952. Born in 1924 in New Jersey, Miss Vaughan sang in church choirs as a girl. In 1942 she entered an amateur contest at New York's Apollo Theater. Singing "Body and Soul," Miss Vaughan not only won the amateur competition, but also attracted the attention of bandleader Earl Hines, who hired her the following year. She joined Billy Eckstine's band in 1944 and a year later began appearing solo. Miss Vaughan's recordings became popular, with "It's Magic" selling over 2 million records. Her other recordings include "Don't Blame Me," "I'm Through With Love," and "I Cover the Waterfront." Miss Vaughan made several singing tours of Europe during the 1950s and 60s.

Wallenstein, Alfred. Considered one of the leading cellists of the U.S. during the 1930s, Alfred Wallenstein became conductor and musical director of the Los Angeles Symphony Orchestra in 1943 and made it one of the outstanding orchestras of the 1940s. Born Alfred von Wallenstein in 1898 in Chicago, he moved at seven with his family to California and at eight began playing cello. Hired as first cellist by the New York Philharmonic Symphony Society in 1929, he became its highest-paid musician. He conducted all-classical network radio programs from 1931 to 1945 and made his debut as symphony conductor in 1932 at the Los Angeles Hollywood Bowl. As conductor of the Los Angeles Symphony, he featured many works by American composers. His network radio program, "Symphonies for Youth," was integrated with classroom study and voted the best educational musical broadcast in 1946 and 1947.

Warfield, William. Acclaimed by music critics in the U.S. and Europe as a leading baritone of the mid-1900s, William Warfield sang the title role in many musical productions, including *Porgy and Bess*. Born in Arkansas in 1920, Warfield studied voice, organ, and piano, and in 1938 he won the vocal competition at the Music Educators National Convention. He attended the Eastman School of Music and the University of Rochester. During World War II, he served in Army Intelligence where his fluency in Italian, French, and German proved invaluable. After the war, Warfield toured with the musical *Call Me Mister*. He made his New York concert debut in 1950. He appeared in motion pictures and on television programs and toured Europe five times for the State Department. Warfield sang with the New York City Opera Company in 1961 and 1964 and was soloist in 1967 with Pablo Casals in Switzerland.

Dionne Warwick **Ethel Waters** **André Watts**

Warwick, Dionne. Considered by many critics to be the leading rhythm and blues singer of the 1960s and 70s, Dionne Warwick appealed to admirers of popular music and gospel singing. Born Marie Dionne Warrick in New Jersey in 1940, Miss Warwick began her singing career with a family gospel choir, the Drinkard Singers, in the early 1950s, and in 1954 she formed, with her sister and cousin, a trio called the Gospelaires. She enrolled at the University of Hartford music school in 1959 to study music education, but her career changed in 1960 when she was chosen by composer Burt Bacharach to record his music. Her records sold millions of copies, and her rendition of Bacharach's "Don't Make Me Over" rose to one of the ten best sellers in the U.S. Miss Warwick toured the U.S. and Europe, appeared in night clubs and on television, and in 1966 made her concert debut in Philharmonic Hall in New York.

Waters, Ethel. Brought up in poverty and an atmosphere of misery, Ethel Waters refused to surrender to her surroundings and later became a popular stage, screen, television, and recording personality of the 20th century. Born in 1900 in Pennsylvania, Miss Waters began singing professionally at 17 in a Baltimore theater. She made her New York debut in the 1927 musical *Africana*. After hearing her sing "Stormy Weather," which later became her song trademark, composer Irving Berlin arranged for her to sing four songs in his 1933 musical, *As Thousands Cheer*. She became the first black actress to be featured in a New York stage drama, *Mamba's Daughters* (1939). Miss Waters's most popular role was in 1940 in the stage musical *Cabin in the Sky*; she was featured in the film version in 1943. She also appeared in the 1949 motion picture *Pinky* and stage and film versions of *The Member of the Wedding* in 1950.

Watts, André. Making his musical debut at 16 as a concert pianist, André Watts won wide acclaim from critics and became the first black musician in the 20th century to appear as soloist at a regular New York Philharmonic Orchestra concert. Born in Germany in 1946, the son of an American career soldier, Watts at age seven began to study piano. Arriving in the U.S. in 1954, he was enrolled at the Philadelphia Musical Academy and later appeared as a soloist at a Philadelphia Orchestra Children's Concert. Watts auditioned with the New York Philharmonic at a Young People's Concert in 1962, and his playing so impressed conductor Leonard Bernstein, that Watts was invited to appear as a substitute soloist. Later Watts gave concerts in Washington, London, and Berlin. He received the 1964 Grammy Award as the most promising classical recording artist. Watts made a world concert tour in 1967.

INDEX
TO MUSICIANS, COMPOSERS, AND SINGERS

A
Anderson, Marian: opera singer, UN delegate, 47
Armstrong, Louis: trumpeter, band leader, 19
Arteaga, Julio de: composer, pianist, 14

B
Bacharach, Burt: composer, 47
Bailey, Pearl: comedienne, singer, 48
Baker, Josephine: internationally known entertainer, 48
Ballard, Louis W.: wrote songs of Indian legends, 48
Basie, Count: created new jazz piano style, 49
Bechet, Sidney: clarinetist in jazz band, 20
Belafonte, Harry: calypso style singer, 49
Berlin, Irving: wrote popular songs for 50 years, 50
Bernstein, Leonard: composer, conductor, 50
Bland, James: wrote "Carry Me Back to Old Virginny," 14
Brice, Fannie: singer and comedienne, 20
Brown, James: recording artist, singer, 51
Burleigh, Harry: composer, 14

C
Cage, John: composer, arranger of unique sounds, 51
Calloway, Cab: singer, actor, band leader, 52
Cantor, Eddie: singer, comedian, entertainer, 20
Capo, Bobby: composer, 52
Cardin, Fred: composer of Indian songs, 52
Carr, Vikki: singer, 53
Carroll, Diahann: singer and actress, 53
Cash, Johnny: country and western singer, 53
Cassadore, Philip: singer of Indian songs, 54
Charles, Ray: pianist, "soul music" singer, 54
Cohan, George M.: actor and composer for 45 years, 15
Cole, Nat "King": singer, 21
Coleman, Ornette: saxophonist, recording artist, 54
Coltrane, John: saxophonist, band leader, 21
Copland, Aaron: award-winning composer, 55
Crosby, Bing: popular singer, actor, 55
Cushman, Charlotte: singer, 7

D
Davis, Miles: trumpeter, band leader, 56
Davis, Sammy, Jr.: singer, dancer, impersonator, 56
Dawson, William L.: composer, conductor, 57
Dett, Robert: composer, 22
Dixon, Dean: conductor of symphony orchestras, 57
Dobbs, Mattiwilda: operatic soprano, 57
Duncan, Todd: actor-singer, voice teacher, 58
Dylan, Bob: folk singer, 58

E
Ellington, Duke: composer, wrote 1,000 tunes, 22
Emmett, Daniel: composer of "Dixie," 7

F
Farrar, Geraldine: operatic soprano, actress, 23
Feliciano, Jose: guitarist, arranger, 8
Fiedler, Arthur: conductor of symphony concerts, 59
Fitzgerald, Ella: popular singer, entertainer, 59
Flores, Pedro: composer, 60
Foster, Stephen: composed many popular ballads, 8
Foy, Eddie: singer, dancer, comedian, 15
Franklin, Aretha: rhythm and blues singer, 60
Fry, William H.: American opera writer, 8

G
Garden, Mary: opera singer, actress, 23
Garland, Judy: singer, actress, 23
Garner, Erroll: internationally known jazz pianist, 61
Gershwin, George: symphonic jazz composer, 24
Gillespie, Dizzy: trumpeter, band leader, 61
Gilmore, Patrick: military band leader, 9
Goodman, Benny: clarinetist, jazz stylist, 61
Greenfield, Elizabeth: soprano, concert artist, 9
Grofe, Ferde: composer, 24
Guthrie, Woody: folk singer, guitarist, composer, 25

H
Hammerstein, Oscar I: grand opera impresario, 15
Hammerstein, Oscar II: wrote lyrics for musicals, 15
Hampton, Lionel: outstanding vibraharpist, 62
Handy, W. C.: cornetist, wrote "St. Louis Blues," 25
Harris, Roy: composer, 62
Hawkins, Coleman: popularized the saxophone, 26
Hayes, Roland: concert tenor, 62
Heifetz, Jascha: violinist, 63
Henderson, Fletcher: pianist, jazz band leader, 26
Henderson, Florence: musical comedy actress, singer, 63
Herbert, Victor: composed light operas, 16
Hernandez, Rafael: wrote Puerto Rican anthem, 26
Hines, Earl: "trumpet style" jazz pianist, 63
Horne, Lena: singer, motion picture actress, 64
Horowitz, Vladimir: pianist, 64
Howe, Julia W.: wrote "Battle Hymn of the Republic," 10

I
Ives, Burl: folk singer, stage and screen actor, 65
Ives, Charles: won Pulitzer Prize for music, 27

J
Jackson, Mahalia: singer of gospel songs, 27
Johnson, J. Rosamond: writer of musical comedies, 28
Johnson, James P.: composer, jazz pianist, 28
Jolson, Al: singer, actor and entertainer, 29
Joplin, Scott: composer of "Maple Leaf Rag," 16

K
Kellogg, Clara Louise: dramatic opera singer, 10
Kern, Jerome: composed many popular songs, 29
King, B. B.: guitarist and blues singer, 65
Kreisler, Fritz: internationally known violinist, 30

L
Lanier, Sidney: writer of poems set to music, 9
Ledbetter, Huddie: composer of folk songs, guitarist, 30
Levant, Oscar: pianist and composer, 30
Lewis, John: arranger, composer, pianist, 65
Lopez, Trini: Latin folk-style singer, 66
Lunceford, Jimmie: orchestra leader, arranger, 31

M
McCormack, John: Irish tenor, concert singer, 31
MacDowell, Edward: pianist, composer, 11
McKuen, Rod: composer and poet, 66
Mathis, Johnny: singer of romantic ballads, 66
Matsumoto, Shigemi: soprano opera singer, 67
Maynor, Dorothy: soprano concert singer, 67
Melchior, Lauritz: Wagnerian tenor, 31
Menotti, Gian-Carlo: composed dramatic operas, 67
Miller, Glenn: popular band leader, 32
Mills, Florence: singer and comedienne, 32
Mitropoulous, Dimitri: symphony orchestra conductor, 32
Monteux, Pierre: conducted more than 60 orchestras, 33
Montgomery, Wes: guitarist, recording artist, 33
Montoya, Carlos: flamenco guitarist, 68
Moore, Grace: opera singer, motion picture actress, 33
Moore, Russell: trombonist, band leader, 68
Morton, Jelly Roll: pianist, jazz composer, 34

N
Nevada, Emma: soprano, opera singer, 34
Nevin, Ethelbert: composed "The Rosary," 11

O
Olcott, Chauncey: singer of Irish songs, 17
Oliver, King: cornet player, band leader, 35
Ormandy, Eugene: conductor of symphony orchestra, 68

P
Paine, John K.: composer of symphonies, 12
Paoli, Antonio: Puerto Rican tenor, 35
Parker, Charlie: outstanding saxophonist, 35
Parker, Horatio: composer, choir director, 12
Peerce, Jan: operatic tenor, concert singer, 69
Peters, Roberta: coloratura soprano, 69
Porter, Cole: composed many popular songs, 36
Powell, Maud: outstanding concert violinist, 17
Presley, Elvis: country and western singer, actor, 69
Price, Leontyne: soprano, opera singer, actress, 70

R
Ritter, Frederic: composer, conductor, 12
Robeson, Paul: singer and stage actor, 70
Rodgers, Richard: composer of many musicals, 71
Rodriguez, Tito: singer, band leader, 36
Rodzinski, Arthur: pianist, conductor, 36
Rosenblatt, Yossele: composed synagogue music, 37
Rubinstein, Artur: concert pianist, 71
Russell, Lillian: comic opera singer, actress, 37

S
Samaroff, Olga: concert pianist, 37
Sanroma, Jesus: symphony orchestra pianist, 38
Schelling, Ernest: pianist, composer, conductor, 38
Schipa, Tito: operatic tenor, 38
Schoenberg, Arnold: wrote unique music style, 39
Schulz, Leo: cellist in leading orchestras, 17
Schuman, William: composer, Pulitzer Prize winner, 72
Schuyler, Philippa: pianist, composer, 39
Seeger, Pete: composer and folk singer, 72
Seidl, Anton: symphony conductor, 13
Serkin, Rudolf: concert pianist, music director, 72
Sills, Beverly: coloratura soprano, 73
Sinatra, Frank: singer and recording artist, 73
Smith, Bessie: popular blues singer, 40
Smith, Kate: popular singer for 40 years, 74
Sousa, John Philip: composer, orchestra leader, 18
Spalding, Albert: internationally known violinist, 40
Stewart, Albert: Indian music singer, 74
Still, William G.: composer, conductor, 74
Stokowski, Leopold: symphony orchestra conductor, 41
Stravinsky, Igor: composer of ballet music, 41
Strube, Gustav: composer of classical music, 42
Suzuki, Pat: singer in many musicals, 75
Swarthout, Gladys: soprano opera singer, 42
Szell, George: symphony orchestra conductor, 43

T
Tatum, Art: pianist, 43
Taylor, Deems: composer, music commentator, 43
Thomas, Theodore: symphony conductor, 13
Thursby, Emma: soprano, 13
Tibbett, Lawrence: baritone opera singer, 44
Traubel, Helen: soprano, 44
Tucker, Richard: operatic tenor, 75

V
Van Heusen, James: wrote popular songs, 75
Varese, Edgar: composer, 44
Vaughan, Sarah: singer, 76

W
Wallenstein, Alfred: cellist, conductor, 76
Waller, Fats: pianist, 45
Walter, Bruno: symphony conductor, 45
Warfield, William: baritone in musicals, 76
Warwick, Dionne: rhythm and blues singer, 77
Waters, Ethel: singer and actress in musicals, 77
Watts, Andre: pianist, 77
White, Clarence: composer, music director, 45
White, Josh: guitarist, folk singer, 46
Whiteman, Paul: orchestra leader, 46

Y
Young, Lester: outstanding saxophonist, 46